Building Secure Software: A Hands-On Guide for Developers

Nikolai Lebedevz

Nikolai Lebedev is an experienced software engineer, security expert, and advocate for secure software practices with over a decade of hands-on experience in designing, developing, and securing applications. Nikolai has worked across diverse industries, helping organizations strengthen their software security posture, from startups to Fortune 500 companies. He combines a deep technical knowledge of coding, cryptography, and system architecture with a pragmatic approach to real-world challenges developers face in today's fast-paced, security-conscious environment.

Passionate about empowering developers to build secure, resilient software, Nikolai has dedicated much of his career to demystifying security practices, making them accessible and actionable for developers at all levels. He has led security training programs, contributed to open-source security tools, and worked closely with DevOps teams to integrate security seamlessly into agile workflows.

In **Building Secure Software: A Hands-On Guide for Developers**, Nikolai brings his unique blend of technical insight, practical guidance, and industry experience to help developers protect their applications against ever-evolving threats. His goal is to provide readers with a comprehensive yet approachable guide to building secure, high-quality software from the ground up.

In a world where digital threats evolve daily, building secure software is no longer an optional skill but a core responsibility for every developer. **Building Secure Software: A Hands-On Guide for Developers** aims to empower developers at all levels to make security a fundamental part of their software development process. This book combines practical, hands-on techniques with the latest insights in secure coding, threat modeling, and DevSecOps, guiding you to create software that's resilient against a wide range of threats.

This guide offers actionable steps to embed security principles at every phase of development, from architecture to deployment. Each chapter covers essential security concepts and best practices, providing the tools you need to design, build, and maintain secure software. With clear explanations, real-world examples, and hands-on exercises, Building Secure Software transforms complex security requirements into manageable and intuitive steps that developers can integrate into their daily workflows.

Chapter 1: Introduction to Secure Software Development

This chapter lays the foundation for understanding software security, exploring its importance in modern development, and introducing core concepts that will recur throughout the book.

Chapter 2: Threat Modeling and Risk Assessment

Dive into threat modeling frameworks and risk assessment techniques to identify, categorize, and prioritize potential threats, enabling you to address security proactively rather than reactively.

Chapter 3: Secure Coding Principles and Best Practices

Learn essential secure coding principles and standards, such as input validation, error handling, and defensive programming, to avoid vulnerabilities in your code.

Chapter 4: Authentication and Access Control

This chapter covers methods for implementing strong authentication and access control systems, including the use of industry standards like OAuth and multi-factor authentication.

Chapter 5: Data Encryption and Storage Security

Discover encryption essentials for securing data at rest and in transit, exploring best practices for hashing, salting, and selecting cryptographic libraries.

Chapter 6: Securing Web Applications

A hands-on look at securing web applications by mitigating common vulnerabilities such as cross-site scripting (XSS), cross-site request forgery (CSRF), and SQL injection.

Chapter 7: API Security and Secure Data Exchange

Explore techniques for securing APIs with authentication, rate limiting, and secure data handling practices to protect against common API security threats.

Chapter 8: Secure Software Design and Architecture

This chapter emphasizes designing security into software architecture, covering principles like least privilege, zero trust, and microservices security.

Chapter 9: Continuous Security in DevOps (DevSecOps)

Learn how to integrate security seamlessly into the CI/CD pipeline, automate security testing, and foster a "shift-left" security culture within DevOps environments.

Chapter 10: Penetration Testing and Code Reviews

Understand the basics of penetration testing and secure code reviews, including static and dynamic analysis, to identify and address vulnerabilities before they're exploited.

Chapter 11: Incident Response and Patch Management

This chapter equips you with strategies for incident response and patch management, ensuring your software remains resilient and up-to-date against new threats.

Chapter 12: Security Challenges and Emerging Threats

An overview of the latest security challenges, from supply chain attacks to AI-driven threats, with guidance on cultivating a security-conscious mindset within development teams.

With **Building Secure Software: A Hands-On Guide for Developers**, you'll gain the skills and confidence to make security an integral part of your software development journey, enabling you to create applications that are robust, resilient, and ready for the digital challenges ahead.

1. Introduction to Secure Software Development

In Introduction to Secure Software Development, we explore why security is a critical element in today's software landscape and introduce core principles that form the foundation for building secure applications. This chapter examines the costs and risks associated with insecure software, from data breaches to damaged reputations, highlighting the importance of proactive security practices. By embedding security into each phase of the software development lifecycle (SDLC), developers can not only protect their applications from common threats but also create a resilient, trustworthy foundation for their software.

1.1 Understanding the Security Landscape: Common Threats and Vulnerabilities

In an increasingly digital world, understanding the security landscape is crucial for developers aiming to build secure software. This chapter delves into the myriad of threats and vulnerabilities that pervade modern applications, providing a comprehensive overview of the risks developers face and the importance of integrating security practices into the software development lifecycle.

The Evolving Threat Landscape

The digital landscape is continuously evolving, influenced by advancements in technology, changes in user behavior, and the growing sophistication of cybercriminals. Threats are no longer limited to traditional malware; they encompass a wide range of tactics, including social engineering, phishing attacks, insider threats, and advanced persistent threats (APTs). Understanding these threats requires a holistic view of the security landscape, recognizing how attackers exploit vulnerabilities in systems, software, and human behavior.

Common Threats in Software Development

Malware: Malware encompasses a variety of malicious software, including viruses, worms, ransomware, and spyware. These programs can disrupt operations, steal sensitive information, and damage systems. For example, ransomware encrypts files and demands payment for decryption, severely impacting organizations' operations.

Developers must consider how to mitigate the risks associated with malware by implementing security measures such as input validation and regular updates.

Phishing: Phishing attacks often use social engineering techniques to trick users into revealing sensitive information, such as passwords and credit card numbers. These attacks can occur through emails, social media, or even phone calls. Understanding how phishing works is crucial for developers, as they need to educate users on recognizing suspicious communications and implementing security features like two-factor authentication (2FA) to provide additional layers of protection.

SQL Injection: SQL injection is a type of attack where malicious SQL code is injected into a query to manipulate databases. This vulnerability arises when user inputs are not properly sanitized, allowing attackers to execute arbitrary SQL commands. Developers can prevent SQL injection by employing parameterized queries and prepared statements, which separate SQL code from user data, ensuring that user inputs cannot alter the intended query structure.

Cross-Site Scripting (XSS): XSS attacks occur when an attacker injects malicious scripts into a web application that is then executed by users' browsers. This can lead to the theft of cookies, session tokens, or other sensitive information. There are three main types of XSS: stored, reflected, and DOM-based. Developers can mitigate XSS vulnerabilities by implementing strict input validation, output encoding, and content security policies (CSP) to limit the execution of unauthorized scripts.

Distributed Denial of Service (DDoS): DDoS attacks aim to overwhelm a target's resources by flooding it with traffic from multiple sources. This can result in service outages, affecting availability and potentially causing reputational damage. Developers should incorporate rate limiting, traffic filtering, and redundant systems to help mitigate the impact of DDoS attacks, ensuring that services remain available even under duress.

Insider Threats: Insider threats stem from individuals within an organization, such as employees or contractors, who intentionally or unintentionally cause harm. This can include data theft, sabotage, or mishandling sensitive information. To combat insider threats, organizations should enforce strict access controls, conduct regular audits, and provide security training to raise awareness about the importance of safeguarding data.

Understanding Vulnerabilities

While threats represent the potential for harm, vulnerabilities are weaknesses in software or systems that attackers can exploit. Recognizing common vulnerabilities is essential for developers to build secure applications.

Input Validation Failures: Failing to validate user inputs can lead to various attacks, including SQL injection and XSS. Developers must implement robust input validation techniques, such as whitelisting acceptable inputs, to ensure that only valid data is processed.

Broken Authentication: Weaknesses in authentication mechanisms can allow unauthorized access to applications. This can arise from poor password policies, lack of account lockout mechanisms, or inadequate session management. Developers should implement strong authentication methods, such as multifactor authentication and secure password storage techniques.

Insecure Direct Object References (IDOR): IDOR occurs when an application exposes direct access to objects based on user input, allowing attackers to access unauthorized resources. For instance, if a URL contains a user ID, an attacker could manipulate this ID to access another user's data. To prevent IDOR, developers should enforce proper authorization checks and avoid exposing direct references to sensitive objects.

Security Misconfiguration: Insecure settings in applications, servers, or cloud environments can lead to vulnerabilities. This can include default credentials, unnecessary services running, or misconfigured security settings. Developers should establish a baseline for secure configurations and conduct regular audits to ensure that systems remain secure.

Sensitive Data Exposure: Applications that do not adequately protect sensitive data, such as personal information, payment details, or health records, are at risk of data breaches. Developers should use encryption for data at rest and in transit, implement strict access controls, and follow data protection regulations to mitigate the risk of exposure.

Insufficient Logging and Monitoring: Without proper logging and monitoring, organizations may struggle to detect and respond to security incidents. Developers should implement comprehensive logging mechanisms and establish alerting systems to monitor for unusual activities, allowing for timely responses to potential threats.

The Importance of Security Awareness

Understanding the security landscape is not solely the responsibility of security professionals; developers play a crucial role in building secure software. Fostering a culture of security awareness within development teams is essential. This involves:

Education and Training: Providing regular security training and workshops helps developers stay informed about current threats and best practices. Awareness of the latest attack vectors empowers developers to proactively incorporate security measures into their work.

Encouraging Security Best Practices: Developers should be encouraged to follow security best practices throughout the software development lifecycle. This includes conducting threat modeling during the design phase, implementing secure coding standards, and participating in code reviews focused on security.

Collaboration with Security Teams: Establishing strong communication and collaboration between development and security teams ensures that security considerations are integrated into every aspect of the development process. Regular meetings and knowledge-sharing sessions can help bridge the gap between these teams.

Understanding the security landscape, including common threats and vulnerabilities, is essential for developers committed to building secure software. By recognizing the various attack vectors and vulnerabilities that can compromise applications, developers can take proactive measures to mitigate risks and enhance the security posture of their software. Integrating security into the development process is not just a technical requirement; it is a fundamental aspect of creating trustworthy applications that users can rely on in an increasingly complex digital world.

1.2 The Cost of Insecurity: Case Studies and Real-World Consequences

In today's interconnected world, the cost of software insecurity extends far beyond the immediate financial impact on a single organization. Security breaches can lead to catastrophic consequences, affecting not only the organization involved but also customers, stakeholders, and even entire industries. This section examines notable case studies that highlight the real-world ramifications of insecure software, providing insights into the potential costs—both tangible and intangible—of neglecting security practices in software development.

Case Study 1: Equifax Data Breach

Overview: In 2017, Equifax, one of the largest credit reporting agencies in the United States, suffered a massive data breach that exposed the personal information of approximately 147 million consumers, including names, Social Security numbers, birth dates, addresses, and, in some cases, driver's license numbers.

Causes: The breach was attributed to a failure to patch a known vulnerability in the Apache Struts web application framework. Although a patch had been released months prior to the breach, Equifax did not apply it in a timely manner.

Consequences:

- **Financial Impact**: Equifax incurred over $4 billion in total costs, including legal fees, settlements, and security improvements. The company allocated $1.4 billion for the costs directly associated with the breach and a projected $2 billion for ongoing security enhancements and legal proceedings.
- **Reputation Damage**: The breach significantly damaged Equifax's reputation. The company's CEO resigned, and public trust eroded, leading to a loss of customers and decreased stock prices.
- **Regulatory Scrutiny**: Equifax faced numerous lawsuits and was subject to investigations by various regulatory bodies. The Federal Trade Commission (FTC) fined Equifax $700 million, and the company agreed to pay up to $425 million to help consumers affected by the breach.

Case Study 2: Target Data Breach

Overview: In late 2013, Target, one of the largest retail chains in the U.S., experienced a data breach that compromised the credit and debit card information of approximately 40 million customers, along with personal information of an additional 70 million customers.

Causes: The breach resulted from the exploitation of network vulnerabilities after attackers gained access through a third-party vendor, Fazio Mechanical Services, which provided HVAC services to Target.

Consequences:

- **Financial Losses**: Target faced costs exceeding $200 million associated with the breach, including settlements, legal fees, and security enhancements.

- **Impact on Sales**: Following the breach, Target experienced a significant decline in sales, particularly during the critical holiday shopping season. The company reported a 46% drop in profits in the fourth quarter of 2013 compared to the previous year.
- **Long-Term Changes**: In response to the breach, Target implemented enhanced security measures, including the adoption of chip-and-PIN technology for card transactions and increased investment in cybersecurity infrastructure.

Case Study 3: Yahoo Data Breach

Overview: Yahoo experienced two major data breaches in 2013 and 2014, compromising the accounts of all three billion user accounts. These breaches were not disclosed until 2016, leading to significant repercussions for the company.

Causes: The breaches were attributed to inadequate security practices, including poor encryption methods and failure to implement effective monitoring and detection systems.

Consequences:

- **Financial Impact**: The breaches ultimately led to a reduction in Yahoo's sale price when Verizon acquired the company in 2017 for $4.48 billion, down from an anticipated $5 billion. Yahoo had to settle for approximately $117.5 million to settle a class-action lawsuit related to the breaches.
- **Loss of Trust**: Yahoo's reputation suffered significantly, with users losing trust in the platform. This erosion of trust hindered Yahoo's ability to attract new users and retain existing ones.
- **Regulatory Actions**: Yahoo faced scrutiny from regulatory bodies, leading to investigations and fines, including a $35 million penalty from the U.S. Securities and Exchange Commission (SEC) for failing to disclose the breach in a timely manner.

Case Study 4: Capital One Data Breach

Overview: In 2019, a former employee of Amazon Web Services (AWS) exploited a misconfigured firewall in Capital One's cloud infrastructure, resulting in the exposure of over 100 million customer accounts and credit applications.

Causes: The breach stemmed from a vulnerability in Capital One's cloud security configuration, which allowed the attacker to access sensitive data stored on AWS.

Consequences:

- **Financial Costs**: Capital One estimated the total costs of the breach to exceed $100 million, including legal fees, regulatory fines, and customer notifications. The company also faced a $80 million fine from the Office of the Comptroller of the Currency (OCC) for its failure to maintain effective risk management.
- **Customer Impact**: The breach compromised sensitive personal data, including Social Security numbers, bank account numbers, and credit scores, affecting customers' privacy and security.
- **Reputation Damage**: Capital One faced significant backlash from customers and stakeholders, damaging its reputation and trustworthiness in the financial sector. The breach led to increased scrutiny regarding cloud security practices within the industry.

The Broader Implications of Insecurity

The case studies above illustrate that the costs of insecurity extend beyond immediate financial losses. The implications of security breaches often ripple throughout organizations and industries, leading to:

Increased Regulatory Pressure: Breaches can trigger heightened regulatory scrutiny, prompting organizations to adopt more stringent security measures and compliance requirements. Non-compliance can result in significant fines and penalties.

Loss of Competitive Advantage: Organizations that suffer breaches may find it challenging to regain their competitive edge. Customers are increasingly cautious about sharing their data with companies that have experienced significant security incidents.

Long-Term Operational Challenges: Security incidents can lead to operational disruptions, diverting resources and focus from core business activities to incident response and remediation efforts. This can slow down innovation and growth.

Market Value Decline: Publicly traded companies often see a decline in stock prices following a breach, as investors react to the potential long-term impact on profitability and reputation. The loss of market value can further exacerbate financial strains on the organization.

Erosion of Customer Trust: Perhaps the most critical consequence of insecurity is the erosion of customer trust. Once customers lose confidence in a brand's ability to protect their data, it can be challenging to rebuild that trust, leading to customer attrition and decreased loyalty.

The cost of insecurity is profound, as evidenced by the case studies of Equifax, Target, Yahoo, and Capital One. These incidents highlight the importance of prioritizing security throughout the software development lifecycle and the necessity of implementing robust security practices. As cyber threats continue to evolve, organizations must remain vigilant, investing in security measures that not only protect their systems but also safeguard customer trust and reputation. Understanding the potential costs of insecurity serves as a powerful motivator for developers and organizations to integrate security into their software development practices, ensuring the creation of resilient applications that can withstand the challenges of today's digital landscape.

1.3 Embedding Security in the Software Development Lifecycle (SDLC)

Incorporating security into the Software Development Lifecycle (SDLC) is essential for building robust and secure applications that can withstand the increasing threat landscape. Traditional approaches to software development often treat security as an afterthought, leading to vulnerabilities that attackers can exploit. By embedding security throughout the SDLC, organizations can proactively address potential risks, reduce vulnerabilities, and foster a culture of security awareness among development teams. This section discusses the key stages of the SDLC and how to integrate security practices effectively at each phase.

Overview of the Software Development Lifecycle (SDLC)

The SDLC consists of several phases, including:

Planning and Requirements Analysis

- Design
- Development
- Testing
- Deployment
- Maintenance

Each of these phases plays a critical role in the overall security posture of the software being developed. Let's explore how security can be embedded into each stage.

1. Planning and Requirements Analysis

Security Integration:

Security Requirements: During the planning phase, it's essential to define security requirements alongside functional requirements. This includes identifying compliance needs, data protection measures, and security controls based on the application's context and the threats it may face.

Threat Modeling: Engage in threat modeling to identify potential threats, vulnerabilities, and attack vectors specific to the application. This process involves analyzing the application's architecture, data flows, and potential entry points for attackers, allowing teams to prioritize security concerns early on.

2. Design

Security Integration:

Secure Architecture: Design the application with security principles in mind. This includes implementing the principle of least privilege, ensuring that users have only the necessary access to perform their tasks. Utilize secure design patterns to address common vulnerabilities, such as using secure communication protocols and implementing authentication and authorization mechanisms effectively.

Data Protection: Ensure that sensitive data is properly handled throughout the design phase. This includes incorporating encryption for data at rest and in transit, as well as identifying any privacy concerns that need to be addressed in compliance with regulations such as GDPR or HIPAA.

3. Development

Security Integration:

Secure Coding Practices: Encourage developers to follow secure coding guidelines and best practices. This involves training developers on common vulnerabilities, such as SQL injection and Cross-Site Scripting (XSS), and providing them with resources, such as the OWASP Top Ten, to help them write secure code.

Static Code Analysis: Implement static code analysis tools that automatically scan the code for vulnerabilities and adherence to secure coding standards. These tools can provide immediate feedback to developers, enabling them to identify and remediate security issues before the code moves to the testing phase.

4. Testing

Security Integration:

Dynamic Application Security Testing (DAST): Conduct DAST to identify vulnerabilities in a running application. This involves simulating real-world attacks to uncover weaknesses that may not be apparent in static analysis. Regular DAST assessments can help identify security issues that arise from configuration or environmental settings.

Penetration Testing: Perform penetration testing as part of the testing phase to evaluate the application's security from an attacker's perspective. Engaging ethical hackers can reveal potential vulnerabilities that automated tools may miss, providing a comprehensive view of the application's security.

Security Testing Frameworks: Integrate security testing frameworks and tools into the overall testing strategy. This could include automated testing for common security issues, ensuring that security tests are part of the continuous integration/continuous deployment (CI/CD) pipeline.

5. Deployment

Security Integration:

Secure Deployment Practices: When deploying the application, utilize secure deployment practices to minimize vulnerabilities. This includes using secure configurations, implementing firewalls, and ensuring that all components of the application are updated with the latest security patches.

Configuration Management: Use configuration management tools to maintain consistent and secure environments. Automating configuration changes can help eliminate human error and ensure that security settings are uniformly applied across development, testing, and production environments.

6. Maintenance

Security Integration:

Ongoing Monitoring: Establish monitoring practices to detect and respond to security incidents in real-time. Implement logging mechanisms to capture relevant security events, and regularly review logs for suspicious activity. This allows organizations to respond swiftly to potential breaches and mitigate damage.

Patch Management: Develop a robust patch management process to ensure that security vulnerabilities are addressed promptly. Regularly review and apply security patches for all software components, including third-party libraries and frameworks.

User Feedback and Incident Response: Encourage users to report any security issues they encounter. Establish a clear incident response plan to address vulnerabilities that may arise post-deployment, ensuring that the organization is prepared to react swiftly to any security threats.

Benefits of Embedding Security in the SDLC

Reduced Vulnerabilities: By addressing security concerns early in the SDLC, organizations can significantly reduce the number of vulnerabilities present in the final product, lowering the risk of security breaches.

Cost Savings: Identifying and fixing security issues during the planning and development phases is generally less costly than addressing them after deployment. Early remediation can save organizations from potential financial losses associated with data breaches, regulatory fines, and damage to reputation.

Increased Collaboration: Embedding security into the SDLC fosters collaboration between development, security, and operations teams (DevSecOps). This collaborative approach enhances communication and understanding of security risks, leading to a more secure overall development process.

Improved Compliance: By incorporating security requirements into the SDLC, organizations can ensure compliance with industry regulations and standards. This not only protects the organization but also builds trust with customers and stakeholders.

Enhanced Customer Trust: Demonstrating a commitment to security throughout the software development process enhances customer trust. When users know that their data is protected, they are more likely to engage with the application and remain loyal to the brand.

Embedding security in the Software Development Lifecycle is not merely a best practice; it is a necessity in today's threat landscape. By integrating security considerations at every stage of the SDLC—from planning and design to development, testing, deployment, and maintenance—organizations can build resilient applications that withstand the evolving challenges of cybersecurity. This proactive approach not only mitigates risks but also fosters a culture of security awareness within development teams, ensuring that security remains a fundamental aspect of the software development process. As the landscape of threats continues to evolve, embedding security in the SDLC will be crucial for safeguarding applications and protecting sensitive data in a digital world.

2. Threat Modeling and Risk Assessment

In Threat Modeling and Risk Assessment, we dive into proactive strategies for identifying, understanding, and prioritizing potential security threats to software systems. This chapter introduces threat modeling frameworks like STRIDE and PASTA, which help developers visualize threats and weaknesses from an attacker's perspective. We also cover risk assessment techniques that categorize threats by their likelihood and impact, providing a structured approach to addressing vulnerabilities efficiently. By integrating threat modeling and risk assessment into the early stages of development, teams can focus their resources on the most critical security risks and build software with robust defenses from the start.

2.1 Overview of Threat Modeling Frameworks (STRIDE, PASTA)

In the realm of cybersecurity, threat modeling is a critical process that helps organizations identify, assess, and prioritize potential threats to their systems and applications. By systematically analyzing the architecture, data flows, and potential vulnerabilities, organizations can develop effective strategies to mitigate risks. Two widely used threat modeling frameworks are STRIDE and PASTA. Each framework offers unique methodologies and benefits, making them suitable for different contexts and applications. This section provides an overview of these two frameworks, highlighting their key features, processes, and applications.

STRIDE Framework

Introduction to STRIDE:

STRIDE is a threat modeling framework developed by Microsoft. The name STRIDE is an acronym that represents six categories of security threats, which helps teams systematically identify potential vulnerabilities in their systems. The framework is particularly effective for identifying threats in software design and architecture.

The Six Categories of STRIDE:

Spoofing: Spoofing refers to an attacker impersonating another user or entity to gain unauthorized access. This can involve tactics such as phishing or using stolen credentials. For example, an attacker might use a legitimate user's credentials to access sensitive data.

Tampering: Tampering involves unauthorized modifications to data or software. An attacker might alter data in transit or change code in an application, potentially leading to data corruption or unauthorized actions. For instance, if an attacker can modify a financial transaction, they could divert funds to their own account.

Repudiation: Repudiation threats occur when a user denies having performed an action, and there is insufficient evidence to prove otherwise. This can be problematic in scenarios where transactions or critical actions need to be tracked. For example, a user might deny making a purchase, leading to disputes.

Information Disclosure: Information disclosure refers to unauthorized access to sensitive information. This can include data breaches where personal data is exposed or leaked. An example is when an application unintentionally reveals user credentials due to improper access controls.

Denial of Service (DoS): Denial of Service threats involve actions that prevent legitimate users from accessing services or resources. This can occur through overwhelming a system with requests, causing it to crash or become unavailable. For example, a DDoS attack floods a server with traffic, rendering it inoperable.

Elevation of Privilege: Elevation of privilege occurs when an attacker gains higher access rights than intended. This can allow them to perform unauthorized actions within a system. For example, a standard user gaining administrative privileges can lead to severe security breaches.

Process of Using STRIDE:

Identify Assets: Start by identifying the critical assets and components within the system, such as data, users, and resources.

Define Security Requirements: Determine the security requirements for each asset, considering confidentiality, integrity, and availability.

Analyze Threats: For each asset, analyze potential threats using the STRIDE categories. Identify which threats apply to each asset and document them.

Prioritize Threats: Assess the likelihood and impact of each threat, allowing for prioritization of which threats need immediate attention.

Mitigation Strategies: Develop and implement strategies to mitigate identified threats, which may include technical controls, policy changes, or user education.

PASTA Framework

Introduction to PASTA:

The Process for Attack Simulation and Threat Analysis (PASTA) framework is a risk-centric threat modeling approach that emphasizes understanding the attacker's perspective. PASTA provides a structured methodology for organizations to simulate potential attacks and assess their impact on assets.

Key Components of PASTA:

Definition of Objectives: The first step in the PASTA process involves defining the business objectives and security goals of the application or system. This includes understanding the critical assets and the potential impact of security incidents on business operations.

Technical Scope: Establishing the technical scope helps to identify the architecture, technologies, and components involved in the system. This step provides context for the subsequent analysis.

Decomposition of the Application: This step involves breaking down the application into its individual components, data flows, and interactions. By analyzing the architecture, teams can identify potential entry points and vulnerabilities.

Threat Analysis: Threat analysis involves identifying potential threats and attack vectors that could target the system. This includes considering both external and internal threats, as well as threat actors' motivations and capabilities.

Vulnerability Analysis: After identifying threats, the next step is to assess the vulnerabilities in the application that could be exploited by attackers. This may involve reviewing code, configurations, and design choices.

Attack Simulation: This phase involves simulating potential attacks based on the identified threats and vulnerabilities. The simulation helps teams understand the potential impact of various attack scenarios and provides insights into the effectiveness of existing security controls.

Risk Assessment: The final step is to assess the risks associated with each identified threat and vulnerability. This includes considering the likelihood of exploitation, the impact of successful attacks, and the effectiveness of current security measures. This assessment helps prioritize remediation efforts.

Benefits of PASTA:

Risk-Centric Approach: PASTA focuses on understanding the risks associated with specific threats and vulnerabilities, allowing organizations to prioritize their security efforts based on business impact.

Emphasis on Attack Simulation: By simulating potential attacks, teams gain valuable insights into real-world attack scenarios, enhancing their ability to prepare for and mitigate risks.

Holistic View: PASTA provides a comprehensive view of the system, considering both technical and business perspectives, which leads to more informed decision-making regarding security measures.

Both STRIDE and PASTA offer valuable frameworks for threat modeling, each catering to different needs and contexts. STRIDE is particularly useful for identifying threats during the design phase, focusing on specific threat categories, while PASTA emphasizes a comprehensive understanding of risk through attack simulation and business impact analysis. By leveraging these frameworks, organizations can improve their threat modeling practices, enhance their security posture, and better protect their applications against potential threats. Ultimately, the choice of framework depends on the specific context of the application, the organization's security goals, and the resources available for threat modeling activities.

2.2 Identifying and Categorizing Threats to Your Application

Identifying and categorizing threats to your application is a critical step in the threat modeling process. Understanding the potential threats that could exploit vulnerabilities allows organizations to develop effective mitigation strategies and enhance the overall security posture of their applications. This section discusses the methods for identifying threats, various threat categories, and best practices for categorization.

Methods for Identifying Threats

Brainstorming Sessions:

Gather cross-functional teams, including developers, security professionals, and business stakeholders, to brainstorm potential threats to the application. Encourage participants to consider various perspectives and think creatively about how threats might manifest.

Reviewing Past Incidents:

Analyze historical security incidents, both within your organization and across the industry. Understanding how previous breaches occurred can provide insights into potential threats and vulnerabilities that may affect your application.

Threat Intelligence Sources:

Leverage external threat intelligence reports, vulnerability databases, and security advisories to identify emerging threats relevant to your application. Sources like the National Vulnerability Database (NVD), Common Vulnerabilities and Exposures (CVE), and industry-specific reports can provide valuable information.

User Stories and Use Cases:

Review user stories and use cases to understand how users interact with the application. Identify potential threats based on user behaviors and the data being processed. This perspective can help uncover threats that might not be apparent from a purely technical viewpoint.

Automated Tools:

Utilize automated threat modeling tools that can analyze your application architecture and identify potential threats. Tools like Microsoft Threat Modeling Tool, OWASP Threat Dragon, and others can help streamline the identification process.

Adopting Frameworks:

Leverage established threat modeling frameworks such as STRIDE and PASTA to guide the identification process. These frameworks provide structured approaches to threat identification, ensuring that critical areas are not overlooked.

Categorizing Threats

Once threats have been identified, it is essential to categorize them to facilitate analysis and prioritization. Threat categorization helps organizations understand the nature and impact of potential threats and develop appropriate response strategies. Below are common threat categories, along with examples:

Malicious Attacks:

These are threats initiated by attackers with the intent to compromise the application, steal data, or disrupt services. Examples include:

- **Denial of Service (DoS):** Overloading the application with traffic to render it unavailable.
- **SQL Injection**: Exploiting input fields to execute unauthorized SQL queries and gain access to the database.

Insider Threats:

Insider threats arise from individuals within the organization who may intentionally or unintentionally cause harm. Examples include:

- **Data Leakage**: Employees inadvertently sharing sensitive information with unauthorized parties.
- **Privilege Abuse**: Authorized users exploiting their access rights to perform unauthorized actions.

Environmental Threats:

Environmental threats encompass risks arising from external conditions that can affect application availability and security. Examples include:

- **Natural Disasters**: Events such as earthquakes, floods, or fires that can disrupt data center operations.
- **Power Failures**: Loss of power that can lead to system outages if not adequately mitigated.

Third-Party Risks:

Third-party risks arise from dependencies on external vendors, services, or components that may introduce vulnerabilities. Examples include:

- **Compromised Libraries**: Using third-party libraries with known vulnerabilities that attackers can exploit.
- **Supply Chain Attacks**: Attackers targeting a third-party vendor to compromise the primary application.

Technical Vulnerabilities:

Technical vulnerabilities are weaknesses in the software or system that can be exploited by attackers. Examples include:

- **Unpatched Software**: Applications or components that have not been updated with the latest security patches.
- **Insecure APIs**: APIs that lack proper authentication and authorization mechanisms, allowing unauthorized access.

Regulatory and Compliance Threats:

These threats arise from failures to comply with industry regulations and standards, leading to legal repercussions. Examples include:

- **Data Breaches**: Violating data protection regulations like GDPR, which can result in significant fines.
- **Audit Failures**: Inability to demonstrate compliance during audits, leading to reputational damage and legal liabilities.

Prioritizing Threats

Once threats have been categorized, it is crucial to prioritize them based on their potential impact and likelihood of occurrence. Prioritization helps organizations focus their resources on addressing the most critical threats first. A commonly used approach for prioritization includes:

Risk Assessment Matrix:

Create a risk assessment matrix to evaluate threats based on their likelihood (probability of occurrence) and impact (potential damage). This can be a simple grid where threats are rated on a scale of low, medium, or high for both dimensions.

Business Impact Analysis:

Assess how each identified threat could affect the business, including financial losses, reputational damage, and operational disruptions. Understanding the business implications can inform prioritization.

Vulnerability Scoring Systems:

Utilize vulnerability scoring systems such as the Common Vulnerability Scoring System (CVSS) to quantify the severity of identified vulnerabilities. This scoring can assist in determining which threats require immediate attention.

Threat Modelling Tools:

Use threat modeling tools that incorporate risk analysis capabilities, allowing teams to visualize and prioritize threats based on various criteria.

Best Practices for Identifying and Categorizing Threats

Regular Updates: Continuously update your threat identification and categorization processes to reflect changes in the application, technology, and threat landscape.

Cross-Functional Collaboration: Involve stakeholders from various teams, including development, security, operations, and business units, to gain diverse perspectives on potential threats.

Document Everything: Maintain thorough documentation of identified threats, their categorization, and prioritization. This documentation can serve as a reference for future assessments and audits.

Review and Refine: Regularly review and refine your threat identification and categorization processes to ensure they remain effective and aligned with organizational goals.

Identifying and categorizing threats to your application is an essential component of the threat modeling process. By employing various methods to uncover potential threats and organizing them into meaningful categories, organizations can better understand the risks they face and prioritize their security efforts effectively. This proactive approach not only enhances the security posture of applications but also ensures that resources are allocated to address the most critical threats, ultimately reducing the likelihood of security incidents and protecting sensitive data. As the threat landscape continues to evolve, maintaining an agile and adaptive threat identification and categorization process will be crucial for safeguarding applications and maintaining user trust.

2.3 Risk Assessment Techniques: Prioritizing and Mitigating Threats

In the ever-evolving landscape of cybersecurity, conducting a thorough risk assessment is essential for identifying, prioritizing, and mitigating threats to your applications. Risk assessment techniques enable organizations to systematically evaluate potential risks, understand their impact, and implement effective strategies to reduce vulnerabilities. This section outlines various risk assessment techniques, their processes, and how they can be applied to prioritize and mitigate threats effectively.

Understanding Risk Assessment

Risk assessment is a structured process that helps organizations identify potential threats, evaluate the likelihood and impact of those threats, and determine appropriate mitigation strategies. The primary goals of risk assessment include:

- **Identifying Risks**: Recognizing potential threats that could affect the organization or its assets.
- **Evaluating Risks**: Assessing the likelihood of each threat occurring and the potential impact on the organization if it does occur.
- **Prioritizing Risks**: Ranking risks based on their severity, enabling organizations to focus on the most critical threats.
- **Mitigating Risks**: Developing and implementing strategies to reduce or eliminate identified risks.

Key Risk Assessment Techniques

Qualitative Risk Assessment

Overview: Qualitative risk assessment relies on subjective judgment to evaluate risks based on descriptive criteria. This technique does not assign numerical values to risks but rather categorizes them as low, medium, or high based on their likelihood and impact.

Process:

- **Identify Risks**: Conduct brainstorming sessions or interviews with stakeholders to identify potential risks.
- **Categorize Risks**: Classify identified risks based on their nature (e.g., technical, operational, regulatory).
- **Assess Likelihood and Impact**: Use scales (e.g., low, medium, high) to evaluate the likelihood of each risk occurring and its potential impact on the organization.
- **Prioritize Risks**: Rank risks based on their assessed likelihood and impact, focusing on those that pose the greatest threat.

Benefits:

- Simple and quick to implement.
- Facilitates discussions among stakeholders to gain consensus on risk perception.

Limitations:

- Subjective judgments can lead to inconsistencies.
- Lack of quantitative data may hinder decision-making in some contexts.

Quantitative Risk Assessment

Overview: Quantitative risk assessment uses numerical values to evaluate risks, allowing for a more objective analysis. This technique often involves calculating potential financial losses, probabilities, and other measurable factors.

Process:

- **Identify Risks**: Similar to qualitative assessments, start by identifying potential risks.
- **Determine Likelihood**: Estimate the probability of each risk occurring, often expressed as a percentage.
- **Calculate Impact**: Assign a monetary value to the potential impact of each risk, such as lost revenue, costs of remediation, or regulatory fines.

Calculate Risk Exposure: Use the formula:

Risk Exposure=Likelihood×Impact

Prioritize Risks: Rank risks based on their calculated risk exposure, allowing organizations to focus on high-risk areas.

Benefits:

- Provides a clear, numerical basis for decision-making.
- Facilitates cost-benefit analyses for risk mitigation strategies.

Limitations:

- Requires accurate data, which may not always be available.
- Can be time-consuming and complex to implement.

Risk Matrix

Overview: A risk matrix is a visual tool that helps organizations assess and prioritize risks based on their likelihood and impact. It provides a clear representation of risk levels, facilitating communication and decision-making.

Process:

- **Define Likelihood and Impact Scales**: Create scales for likelihood (e.g., rare, unlikely, likely, almost certain) and impact (e.g., insignificant, minor, moderate, major, catastrophic).
- **Plot Risks**: Place identified risks on the matrix based on their assessed likelihood and impact.
- **Determine Risk Level**: Identify risk levels (e.g., low, medium, high) based on their position on the matrix.
- **Prioritize Risks**: Focus on high-level risks that require immediate attention.

Benefits:

- Provides a visual representation of risks for easier understanding.
- Facilitates discussions and consensus among stakeholders.

Limitations:

- May oversimplify complex risk scenarios.
- Subjectivity in risk placement can lead to inconsistencies.

Bowtie Analysis

Overview: Bowtie analysis is a risk assessment technique that visually represents the relationship between potential threats and their consequences. It provides a comprehensive view of risks and their controls.

Process:

- **Identify Hazards**: Determine potential hazards that could lead to undesirable events.
- **Identify Threats and Consequences**: For each hazard, identify potential threats and their potential consequences.
- **Develop Controls**: Identify preventive controls (to mitigate threats) and recovery controls (to minimize consequences).
- **Visual Representation**: Create a bowtie diagram that illustrates the relationship between hazards, threats, consequences, and controls.

Benefits:

- Provides a clear visual representation of risk management strategies.
- Encourages proactive thinking about both prevention and recovery.

Limitations:

- May require significant time and resources to develop.
- Complexity may overwhelm smaller teams.

Scenario Analysis

Overview: Scenario analysis involves creating hypothetical scenarios to explore how specific risks could manifest and their potential impact on the organization. This technique allows teams to evaluate the effectiveness of mitigation strategies.

Process:

- **Identify Key Risks**: Identify critical risks to analyze.

- **Develop Scenarios**: Create detailed scenarios based on potential risk events.
- **Evaluate Impacts**: Assess the potential consequences of each scenario, including financial, operational, and reputational impacts.
- **Identify Mitigation Strategies**: Evaluate existing controls and identify additional measures that could mitigate the risks.

Benefits:

- Provides insights into real-world implications of risks.
- Encourages creative thinking and collaboration among stakeholders.

Limitations:

- May be time-consuming to develop detailed scenarios.
- Subjectivity in scenario development can lead to inconsistencies.

Mitigating Threats

After identifying and prioritizing risks, organizations must develop and implement strategies to mitigate those threats effectively. Mitigation strategies can include:

Implementing Security Controls:

Deploy technical controls such as firewalls, intrusion detection systems, encryption, and access controls to protect against identified threats.

Policy Development:

Establish clear security policies and procedures that define acceptable use, incident response, and compliance requirements. Ensure that all employees are trained on these policies.

Regular Security Audits:

Conduct regular security audits and assessments to identify new vulnerabilities and ensure that existing controls remain effective.

Incident Response Planning:

Develop and maintain an incident response plan that outlines procedures for detecting, responding to, and recovering from security incidents.

Continuous Monitoring:

Implement continuous monitoring of systems and networks to detect anomalies and potential threats in real-time.

User Education and Awareness:

Educate employees about security best practices and the importance of vigilance in recognizing potential threats, such as phishing attacks or social engineering tactics.

Regular Updates and Patching:

Ensure that software and systems are kept up to date with the latest security patches to reduce vulnerabilities.

Risk assessment is a crucial component of an effective cybersecurity strategy. By employing various techniques to identify, categorize, and prioritize risks, organizations can develop a comprehensive understanding of potential threats to their applications. This knowledge allows for targeted mitigation strategies that enhance the security posture and resilience of the organization. Continuous risk assessment and proactive threat mitigation will be essential as the threat landscape evolves and new challenges emerge. Organizations that prioritize risk assessment will be better positioned to protect their applications, safeguard sensitive data, and maintain user trust.

3. Secure Coding Principles and Best Practices

In Secure Coding Principles and Best Practices, we cover essential guidelines and techniques to prevent vulnerabilities and enhance code security. This chapter introduces widely recognized standards, such as those from OWASP and CWE, that help developers write defensively and avoid common coding pitfalls. Key practices include input validation, error handling, and secure data storage, all aimed at protecting applications from threats like injection attacks and unauthorized access. By adopting secure coding principles early in the development process, developers can significantly reduce security risks, creating code that is resilient, reliable, and less susceptible to exploitation.

3.1 Fundamental Secure Coding Standards (OWASP, CWE, SANS)

In an age where software vulnerabilities can lead to significant security breaches, establishing and adhering to secure coding standards is paramount. These standards provide developers with guidelines and best practices to build applications that are resilient against various forms of attack. Among the most recognized organizations that contribute to secure coding standards are the Open Web Application Security Project (OWASP), the Common Weakness Enumeration (CWE), and the SANS Institute. This section explores the fundamental secure coding standards provided by these organizations, their importance, and practical applications in software development.

1. OWASP Secure Coding Standards

Overview:

OWASP is a nonprofit organization dedicated to improving the security of software. The OWASP Secure Coding Practices document outlines essential principles and best practices for writing secure code across various programming languages.

Key Principles:

Input Validation: Ensure all inputs are validated against expected formats, types, and lengths to prevent injection attacks and other vulnerabilities.

Output Encoding: Encode outputs to prevent cross-site scripting (XSS) attacks. This involves converting potentially dangerous characters into a safe format before rendering them in the browser.

Authentication and Session Management: Implement strong authentication mechanisms and manage sessions securely. This includes using secure passwords, multifactor authentication, and proper session expiration policies.

Access Control: Enforce the principle of least privilege by ensuring users have access only to the resources they need. Implement robust authorization mechanisms to validate user permissions.

Error Handling and Logging: Ensure that error messages do not reveal sensitive information about the application. Implement logging to capture security events for auditing and forensic analysis.

Data Protection: Encrypt sensitive data both in transit and at rest. Use strong encryption standards and manage cryptographic keys securely.

Configuration Management: Securely configure servers and applications. Disable unnecessary features and services, and enforce secure defaults.

Secure Communication: Use secure communication protocols (e.g., HTTPS, TLS) to protect data transmitted over networks.

Implementation:

Developers should integrate OWASP Secure Coding Practices into their development workflow. This involves training, code reviews, and automated tools that enforce these standards throughout the software development lifecycle (SDLC).

2. Common Weakness Enumeration (CWE)

Overview:

CWE is a community-developed list of common software and hardware weaknesses. It provides a framework for identifying and mitigating vulnerabilities in software. The CWE list categorizes weaknesses, making it easier for developers to understand and address them.

Key Categories:

Injection Flaws (CWE-77): Issues like SQL injection and command injection that occur when untrusted data is sent to an interpreter. Mitigation involves proper input validation and parameterized queries.

Improper Authentication (CWE-287): Weak authentication mechanisms that can be exploited to bypass security controls. Solutions include enforcing strong password policies and implementing multifactor authentication.

Sensitive Data Exposure (CWE-200): Weaknesses that allow sensitive information to be accessed by unauthorized users. Use strong encryption and secure storage practices to mitigate this risk.

Cross-Site Scripting (CWE-79): A vulnerability that allows attackers to inject malicious scripts into web pages viewed by other users. Proper output encoding and input validation can help prevent this.

Insecure Configuration (CWE-16): Weak configurations that expose systems to attacks. Regularly audit and harden system configurations to minimize exposure.

Implementation:

Developers can use the CWE list to perform code reviews, identify potential weaknesses, and apply the recommended mitigation strategies. Incorporating CWE awareness into development training helps raise security consciousness among development teams.

3. SANS Institute Secure Coding Standards

Overview:

The SANS Institute is a global leader in cybersecurity training and education. The SANS Secure Coding Standards provide guidelines for writing secure code in various programming languages. SANS emphasizes practical implementation and covers multiple languages, including Java, C/C++, and Python.

Key Principles:

Secure Programming Practices: Follow secure programming practices specific to the programming language being used. For instance, use safe string functions in C/C++ to prevent buffer overflows.

Data Validation and Sanitization: Implement strict data validation and sanitization techniques to protect against injection attacks and other vulnerabilities.

Use of Security Libraries and Frameworks: Leverage established security libraries and frameworks that have been vetted for vulnerabilities. This can save time and effort while ensuring robust security.

Regular Security Testing: Integrate security testing into the development lifecycle, including static and dynamic analysis, penetration testing, and vulnerability scanning.

Security Training and Awareness: Provide developers with ongoing training in secure coding practices. Regular workshops and courses can keep developers informed about the latest threats and mitigations.

Implementation:

Organizations can adopt the SANS Secure Coding Standards by conducting training sessions for developers and incorporating the guidelines into their coding practices. Additionally, organizations should ensure that these standards are integrated into their security policies and procedures.

The Importance of Secure Coding Standards

Adhering to secure coding standards is critical for several reasons:

Minimizing Vulnerabilities: Secure coding standards help developers identify and mitigate common vulnerabilities, reducing the attack surface of applications.

Improving Code Quality: Implementing best practices leads to higher code quality, making applications more maintainable and less prone to bugs.

Regulatory Compliance: Many industries require adherence to specific security standards. Following secure coding standards can help organizations meet compliance requirements and avoid legal penalties.

Building User Trust: Applications that are secure foster trust among users, leading to higher adoption rates and customer satisfaction.

Reducing Long-term Costs: By addressing security concerns during development, organizations can avoid the significant costs associated with security breaches, including remediation, legal fees, and reputational damage.

Secure coding standards established by OWASP, CWE, and SANS provide a comprehensive framework for developing secure software. By adhering to these guidelines, developers can identify common vulnerabilities, implement best practices, and create applications that are resilient against potential attacks. Establishing a culture of security within development teams, along with ongoing training and assessment, will further enhance the security posture of organizations. As the threat landscape continues to evolve, integrating secure coding standards into the software development lifecycle will be essential for protecting sensitive data and maintaining user trust.

3.2 Avoiding Common Coding Pitfalls and Anti-Patterns

In software development, certain practices can inadvertently introduce vulnerabilities or reduce the overall security posture of an application. These practices, often referred to as "coding pitfalls" or "anti-patterns," can lead to serious consequences if not addressed. Understanding these common pitfalls is crucial for developers who aim to write secure code and create resilient applications. This section explores prevalent coding pitfalls, their implications, and strategies for avoiding them.

1. Hardcoding Secrets

Description:

Hardcoding sensitive information, such as passwords, API keys, or cryptographic keys directly into source code, is a prevalent pitfall. This practice compromises security, especially if the code is shared publicly or stored in version control systems without adequate protections.

Implications:

- **Exposed Credentials**: Hardcoded secrets can be easily discovered by malicious actors, leading to unauthorized access to systems or data.

- **Difficulty in Key Management**: Changing hardcoded values requires code modifications and redeployments, complicating key rotation practices.

Avoidance Strategies:

- **Use Environment Variables**: Store sensitive data in environment variables instead of hardcoding them in the application. This separates secrets from the codebase.
- **Configuration Files**: Utilize external configuration files with restricted access to manage sensitive information. Ensure these files are not included in version control.
- **Secrets Management Tools**: Leverage dedicated secrets management tools (e.g., HashiCorp Vault, AWS Secrets Manager) to securely store and retrieve sensitive data.

2. Lack of Input Validation

Description:

Failing to validate user inputs is a common pitfall that can lead to various vulnerabilities, including SQL injection, cross-site scripting (XSS), and buffer overflows.

Implications:

- **Injection Attacks**: Unsanitized inputs can allow attackers to execute malicious code or queries.
- **Application Crashes**: Invalid inputs may cause applications to behave unpredictably or crash.

Avoidance Strategies:

- **Whitelist Validation**: Use a whitelist approach to validate inputs against a predefined set of acceptable values. Reject any input that does not meet the criteria.
- **Regular Expressions**: Employ regular expressions to enforce input formats, ensuring that only valid data is accepted.
- **Sanitize Inputs**: Properly sanitize and encode inputs before processing or storing them to mitigate injection risks.

3. Insecure Error Handling

Description:

Insecure error handling occurs when applications display detailed error messages to end users. These messages can provide valuable information to attackers about the application's structure and potential weaknesses.

Implications:

- **Information Leakage**: Detailed error messages can expose stack traces, database queries, or application logic, facilitating further attacks.
- **User Confusion**: Users may become confused or frustrated when presented with unhelpful error messages.

Avoidance Strategies:

- **Generic Error Messages**: Implement generic error messages for end users, avoiding specific details about the underlying system. For example, use "An error occurred. Please try again later." instead of disclosing technical details.
- **Logging Errors**: Log detailed error information internally for developers to review while ensuring logs do not expose sensitive data.
- **Monitoring and Alerting**: Implement monitoring and alerting systems to detect and respond to errors and anomalies without revealing sensitive information to users.

4. Failure to Use Parameterized Queries

Description:

Using dynamic queries constructed with user input can lead to SQL injection vulnerabilities. This pitfall arises when developers concatenate user inputs directly into SQL statements.

Implications:

- **Database Compromise**: Attackers can manipulate queries to execute arbitrary SQL commands, leading to data exposure, modification, or deletion.
- **Data Integrity Risks**: Malicious inputs can corrupt data integrity, resulting in unintended consequences.

Avoidance Strategies:

- **Parameterized Queries**: Always use parameterized queries or prepared statements to separate SQL logic from data, ensuring user inputs are treated as data rather than executable code.
- **ORM Frameworks**: Utilize Object-Relational Mapping (ORM) frameworks that inherently use parameterized queries to reduce the risk of SQL injection.
- **Input Sanitization**: While parameterized queries are crucial, always sanitize inputs as an additional layer of security.

5. Poor Session Management

Description:

Ineffective session management can lead to session fixation, session hijacking, and unauthorized access. Common issues include predictable session IDs, lack of expiration policies, and improper handling of session tokens.

Implications:

- **Account Takeover**: Attackers can gain access to user accounts by hijacking sessions or exploiting predictable session identifiers.
- **Data Breaches**: Poor session management can result in unauthorized access to sensitive data or actions.

Avoidance Strategies:

- **Use Secure Cookies**: Set the HttpOnly and Secure flags on cookies to prevent client-side scripts from accessing session tokens and ensure they are transmitted only over HTTPS.
- **Implement Session Expiration**: Enforce session expiration policies, automatically logging users out after a defined period of inactivity.
- **Regenerate Session IDs**: Regenerate session IDs upon authentication and sensitive actions to mitigate session fixation risks.

6. Inadequate Logging and Monitoring

Description:

Insufficient logging and monitoring practices can hinder the detection of security incidents, making it challenging to respond effectively to breaches or attacks.

Implications:

- **Delayed Incident Response**: Without adequate logs, identifying and responding to security incidents may be delayed, increasing the potential impact.
- **Lack of Accountability**: Incomplete logging may prevent organizations from attributing actions to specific users or identifying patterns of malicious activity.

Avoidance Strategies:

- **Comprehensive Logging**: Implement logging for critical events, including authentication attempts, access to sensitive data, and changes to user roles or permissions.
- **Centralized Logging**: Use centralized logging solutions (e.g., ELK Stack, Splunk) to aggregate logs for easier analysis and monitoring.
- **Regular Reviews**: Conduct regular log reviews and audits to identify anomalies and ensure logging practices are maintained.

7. Ignoring Security Updates

Description:

Failing to apply security patches and updates can leave applications vulnerable to known exploits. Many developers neglect this critical aspect of software maintenance, believing their applications are secure without regular updates.

Implications:

- **Exposure to Exploits**: Known vulnerabilities in libraries or frameworks can be exploited by attackers, leading to data breaches or service disruptions.
- **Increased Technical Debt**: Delayed updates can lead to significant technical debt, making future updates more complex and time-consuming.

Avoidance Strategies:

- **Establish a Patch Management Process**: Create a routine for monitoring and applying security updates for libraries, frameworks, and the underlying infrastructure.

- **Automated Tools**: Use automated tools (e.g., Dependabot, Snyk) to alert developers about outdated dependencies and known vulnerabilities.
- **Security Assessments**: Conduct regular security assessments and code reviews to identify and remediate outdated components.

Avoiding common coding pitfalls and anti-patterns is essential for developing secure software. By understanding these pitfalls and implementing best practices, developers can significantly reduce vulnerabilities in their applications. Establishing a culture of security within development teams, providing ongoing training, and integrating security into the software development lifecycle (SDLC) will further enhance the security posture of organizations. As the threat landscape continues to evolve, staying vigilant and proactive in identifying and mitigating coding pitfalls will be critical to ensuring the resilience and integrity of software applications.

3.3 Implementing Defensive Programming Techniques

Defensive programming is a proactive approach to software development that focuses on anticipating potential errors and vulnerabilities in code. By employing defensive programming techniques, developers can create applications that are more robust, secure, and resilient to unexpected input or malicious attacks. This section explores the key principles and techniques of defensive programming, emphasizing their significance in enhancing software security and reliability.

1. Input Validation and Sanitization

Description:

Input validation is the practice of ensuring that user inputs conform to predefined rules before processing. This technique helps prevent attacks such as SQL injection, cross-site scripting (XSS), and buffer overflows by rejecting malicious or unexpected data.

Implementation Techniques:

Whitelist Validation: Use a whitelist approach, allowing only known good inputs. This is more secure than a blacklist approach, which attempts to filter out known bad inputs. For example, if expecting an email address, validate it against a regex pattern that matches standard email formats.

Type Checking: Ensure that inputs match expected types (e.g., integers, strings) before processing. In languages with strong typing, leverage the type system to enforce type safety.

Sanitize Inputs: Clean user inputs by removing or encoding potentially dangerous characters. For instance, in web applications, encode outputs to prevent XSS attacks by converting special characters like < and > into their HTML entity equivalents.

2. Using Assertions

Description:

Assertions are statements in code that check for expected conditions during execution. They serve as a debugging aid by verifying assumptions made by the programmer, and can help catch errors early in the development process.

Implementation Techniques:

Preconditions: Use assertions to validate preconditions before executing critical code segments. For example, assert that a function receives valid parameters before proceeding with calculations.

Postconditions: After executing a function, use assertions to check that the expected outcomes are met. This ensures that the function behaves as intended.

Invariants: Implement assertions to maintain invariants within data structures or classes, ensuring that certain conditions hold true throughout the lifecycle of an object.

3. Error Handling

Description:

Effective error handling is essential in defensive programming. Instead of allowing an application to crash or behave unpredictably, developers should implement robust error-handling mechanisms to gracefully manage unexpected situations.

Implementation Techniques:

Use Exception Handling: Implement try-catch blocks to handle exceptions gracefully. This allows developers to respond to errors appropriately, log relevant information, and provide users with meaningful feedback.

Fail Early and Loudly: Detect and report errors as early as possible. Use assertions and logging to capture error details for debugging, ensuring that developers can quickly address issues before they escalate.

User-Friendly Error Messages: Provide users with clear, non-technical error messages while logging detailed information for developers. This ensures users understand the issue without revealing sensitive application details.

4. Resource Management

Description:

Proper resource management is crucial for preventing resource leaks, which can lead to performance degradation, application crashes, or denial of service. Defensive programming techniques help ensure that resources are allocated and released appropriately.

Implementation Techniques:

Use RAII (Resource Acquisition Is Initialization): In languages like C++, use RAII principles to ensure that resources are automatically released when they go out of scope. This approach minimizes the risk of resource leaks.

Explicitly Release Resources: In languages without automatic memory management (e.g., C), explicitly free memory and release file handles or database connections when they are no longer needed.

Monitor Resource Usage: Implement logging and monitoring to track resource usage, allowing developers to identify potential leaks or bottlenecks in the application.

5. Code Reviews and Pair Programming

Description:

Conducting code reviews and practicing pair programming are effective defensive programming techniques that promote collaborative coding and knowledge sharing among team members.

Implementation Techniques:

Regular Code Reviews: Implement a structured code review process where team members review each other's code for potential vulnerabilities, adherence to coding standards, and overall quality. This practice enhances code quality and helps catch issues before deployment.

Pair Programming: Pair programming involves two developers working together at the same workstation. One writes code while the other reviews it in real-time, fostering immediate feedback and collaboration.

Use Checklists: Create checklists for code reviews that include security considerations, common coding pitfalls, and best practices to ensure comprehensive evaluations.

6. Logging and Monitoring

Description:

Incorporating logging and monitoring into applications is crucial for defensive programming. Effective logging helps developers track application behavior, identify potential issues, and respond to security incidents.

Implementation Techniques:

Log Security Events: Log significant security-related events, such as authentication attempts, access to sensitive data, and configuration changes. Ensure logs contain sufficient context for troubleshooting and analysis.

Implement Log Rotation and Retention Policies: Regularly rotate logs to prevent excessive disk usage and implement retention policies to determine how long logs are stored.

Monitor Logs for Anomalies: Use automated monitoring tools to analyze logs for unusual patterns or suspicious activity, enabling timely responses to potential security incidents.

7. Continuous Security Testing

Description:

Defensive programming extends beyond coding practices; it encompasses the continuous testing of applications for vulnerabilities. Regular security assessments help identify weaknesses that could be exploited by attackers.

Implementation Techniques:

Static Analysis Tools: Integrate static code analysis tools into the development pipeline to automatically scan code for known vulnerabilities and coding issues. These tools help catch issues early in the development lifecycle.

Dynamic Analysis and Penetration Testing: Conduct dynamic analysis and penetration testing to identify vulnerabilities in running applications. Regular assessments help uncover potential attack vectors and provide insights for remediation.

Continuous Integration/Continuous Deployment (CI/CD): Incorporate security testing into CI/CD pipelines to ensure that security checks are performed automatically with each code change, enabling rapid identification of vulnerabilities.

Implementing defensive programming techniques is essential for building secure and resilient applications. By proactively addressing potential vulnerabilities and anticipating unexpected input, developers can create software that withstands a wide range of threats. The combination of input validation, error handling, resource management, and continuous security testing forms a robust defensive programming strategy. As threats evolve, adopting these techniques will enhance the security posture of software applications and protect sensitive data from unauthorized access and exploitation. By fostering a culture of security awareness and collaboration among development teams, organizations can ensure that their applications are not only functional but also secure.

4. Authentication and Access Control

In Authentication and Access Control, we explore the critical mechanisms that safeguard user identities and ensure that only authorized individuals can access sensitive resources. This chapter delves into robust authentication methods, including multi-factor authentication (MFA), OAuth, and OpenID Connect, highlighting their importance in creating secure user experiences. We also discuss the principles of access control, focusing on role-based access control (RBAC) and attribute-based access control (ABAC) to manage permissions effectively. By implementing strong authentication and finely-tuned access control measures, developers can protect their applications against unauthorized access and ensure that user data remains secure, fostering trust in their systems.

4.1 Strong Authentication Mechanisms (OAuth, OpenID Connect)

Authentication is a critical component of security in software applications, serving as the gateway to user access and data protection. As threats evolve, implementing strong authentication mechanisms has become essential to safeguard sensitive information and ensure that only authorized users can access specific resources. This section focuses on two widely used authentication protocols: OAuth and OpenID Connect, exploring their features, differences, and implementation considerations.

1. Understanding OAuth

Overview:

OAuth (Open Authorization) is an open standard for access delegation commonly used as a way to grant websites or applications limited access to user information without exposing passwords. It enables a third-party application to obtain limited access to a user's resources hosted on another service.

How It Works:

Roles in OAuth: OAuth defines several roles:

- **Resource Owner**: The user who owns the data and grants access to it.

- **Client**: The application requesting access to the resource owner's data.
- **Authorization Server**: The server that authenticates the resource owner and issues access tokens to the client.
- **Resource Server**: The server hosting the resource owner's data, which accepts and responds to requests using access tokens.

Authorization Flow: The OAuth authorization process generally follows these steps:

- **Authorization Request**: The client requests authorization from the resource owner, typically by redirecting the user to the authorization server.
- **Authorization Grant**: The resource owner grants authorization (often via a user interface) and provides an authorization grant to the client.
- **Access Token Request**: The client exchanges the authorization grant for an access token by making a request to the authorization server.
- **Access Token Response**: The authorization server validates the grant and returns an access token to the client.
- **Resource Access**: The client uses the access token to access the resource owner's data from the resource server.

Use Cases:

OAuth is commonly used in scenarios where applications need to access resources on behalf of users without directly sharing passwords. Examples include allowing users to log in to a third-party application using their Google or Facebook accounts.

2. Understanding OpenID Connect

Overview:

OpenID Connect is a simple identity layer on top of the OAuth 2.0 protocol. While OAuth provides authorization, OpenID Connect adds authentication to the mix, enabling applications to verify the identity of users based on the authentication performed by an authorization server.

How It Works:

Core Components: OpenID Connect introduces additional components:

- **ID Token**: A JSON Web Token (JWT) that contains user information, including the user's identity and authentication status.

- **User Info Endpoint**: An endpoint that the client can call to obtain additional user profile information.

Authentication Flow: The OpenID Connect flow typically follows these steps:

- **Authentication Request**: Similar to OAuth, the client redirects the user to the authorization server for authentication.
- **User Authentication**: The resource owner authenticates (e.g., via username/password, biometrics) on the authorization server.
- **Authorization Grant and ID Token**: Upon successful authentication, the authorization server provides both an ID token and an authorization code.
- **Token Exchange**: The client exchanges the authorization code for an access token and an ID token.
- **User Info Retrieval**: The client can optionally retrieve additional user information from the User Info Endpoint.

Use Cases:

OpenID Connect is commonly used for single sign-on (SSO) scenarios, where users can authenticate once and gain access to multiple applications or services without needing to log in again.

3. Key Features and Benefits

Strong Security:

Both OAuth and OpenID Connect employ industry-standard security practices, such as token-based authentication and scopes, which limit access to only the necessary resources.

User Experience:

These protocols enhance user experience by enabling SSO capabilities, allowing users to authenticate once and access multiple services without repeatedly entering credentials.

Delegated Access:

OAuth allows users to grant third-party applications limited access to their data without sharing passwords, improving security while maintaining usability.

Scalability:

OAuth and OpenID Connect are designed to scale with applications, supporting a wide range of authentication scenarios, including mobile, web, and IoT applications.

4. Implementation Considerations

Choosing the Right Flow:

Depending on the application type, developers should choose the appropriate OAuth 2.0 flow (e.g., Authorization Code Flow, Implicit Flow, Client Credentials Flow) that aligns with security and usability requirements.

Secure Token Storage:

Tokens should be securely stored on the client side (e.g., using secure cookies or local storage) and should be transmitted only over secure channels (HTTPS).

Scope Management:

Implement fine-grained scopes to limit access to specific resources based on user permissions, ensuring that clients only receive the minimum necessary access.

Regular Token Rotation:

Implement mechanisms for token rotation and revocation to reduce the risk associated with stolen tokens. Access tokens should have short lifetimes, and refresh tokens can be used to obtain new access tokens without requiring user interaction.

User Consent:

Clearly communicate to users what data is being accessed and how it will be used. Obtaining explicit user consent is a best practice that enhances trust.

Strong authentication mechanisms like OAuth and OpenID Connect play a vital role in securing applications and protecting user data. By providing robust, flexible, and user-friendly authentication options, these protocols enable developers to create applications that meet modern security requirements while enhancing user experiences. Implementing these mechanisms effectively requires careful consideration of flows, security practices, and user consent, but the resulting improvements in security and usability are well worth the effort. As organizations increasingly rely on web and mobile applications, adopting OAuth and OpenID Connect can significantly bolster their security posture and protect sensitive information from unauthorized access.

4.2 Implementing Role-Based and Attribute-Based Access Control (RBAC, ABAC)

Access control is a fundamental aspect of software security, ensuring that only authorized users can access certain resources or perform specific actions within an application. Two widely adopted access control models are Role-Based Access Control (RBAC) and Attribute-Based Access Control (ABAC). This section will explore the principles, implementation strategies, and use cases for RBAC and ABAC, highlighting their strengths and considerations for deployment.

1. Role-Based Access Control (RBAC)

Overview:

RBAC is a widely used access control model that assigns permissions to users based on their roles within an organization. A role represents a collection of permissions, and users can be assigned to one or more roles, simplifying permission management.

Core Concepts:

Roles: Defined sets of permissions that dictate what actions a user can perform within an application. Examples include "Admin," "Editor," and "Viewer."

Users: Individual accounts that are assigned one or more roles. A user inherits the permissions associated with their roles.

Permissions: Specific access rights or operations that can be performed, such as "Create Document," "Edit Document," or "Delete Document."

How It Works:

Role Assignment: Users are assigned to roles based on their job responsibilities or functions. For example, a manager might have an "Admin" role, while a regular employee may have a "Viewer" role.

Access Control Decisions: When a user attempts to perform an action, the system checks their assigned roles against the required permissions for that action. If the user's roles include the necessary permissions, access is granted.

Advantages of RBAC:

Simplicity: RBAC simplifies permission management, making it easy to add or remove users from roles without needing to change individual permissions.

Least Privilege Principle: By assigning roles based on job functions, RBAC helps enforce the principle of least privilege, minimizing unnecessary access to sensitive data.

Scalability: RBAC scales well in larger organizations where managing permissions on an individual basis would be impractical.

Challenges of RBAC:

Role Explosion: In complex organizations, the number of roles can grow significantly, leading to difficulties in management and potential overlaps in permissions.

Static Permissions: RBAC typically does not account for contextual factors, such as time of access or resource sensitivity, which may be important for making dynamic access decisions.

2. Attribute-Based Access Control (ABAC)

Overview:

ABAC is a more flexible and dynamic access control model that makes access decisions based on attributes associated with users, resources, and the environment. Attributes can be user-specific (e.g., role, department), resource-specific (e.g., document type, sensitivity), and contextual (e.g., time of access, location).

Core Concepts:

Attributes: Characteristics that define users, resources, and environment conditions. Examples include user roles, department, resource classification, and time of access.

Policies: Rules that define access decisions based on the evaluation of attributes. Policies specify which attributes must be present for access to be granted.

Policies Evaluation: The process of assessing whether a user meets the defined access requirements based on their attributes and the attributes of the resource they are trying to access.

How It Works:

Attribute Definition: Define the relevant attributes for users, resources, and the environment. For example, an attribute for a user might be "Department: HR," while a resource attribute might be "Sensitivity: Confidential."

Policy Creation: Create policies that specify which attributes must be present for access to be granted. For instance, "Allow access to confidential documents only for users in the HR department during business hours."

Access Control Decisions: When a user attempts to access a resource, the system evaluates their attributes against the relevant policies. Access is granted or denied based on whether the policies are satisfied.

Advantages of ABAC:

Flexibility: ABAC allows for fine-grained access control based on a wide range of attributes, accommodating dynamic access requirements and contextual factors.

Dynamic Policy Enforcement: Access decisions can change based on varying conditions, providing a more adaptable security model that can respond to specific contexts.

Reduced Role Explosion: By leveraging attributes instead of roles, ABAC can minimize the proliferation of roles, simplifying management.

Challenges of ABAC:

Complexity: The management of attributes and policies can become complex, especially in large organizations with many resources and users.

Performance: Evaluating policies based on multiple attributes may introduce performance overhead, particularly if not designed efficiently.

3. Implementation Strategies

Choosing Between RBAC and ABAC:

The decision to implement RBAC or ABAC should be guided by the organization's specific needs:

RBAC is suitable for environments with well-defined roles and straightforward permission structures, where the complexity of managing roles is manageable.

ABAC is ideal for scenarios requiring fine-grained access control and where context plays a significant role in access decisions, such as regulatory environments or dynamic applications.

Integration Considerations:

User Management: Implement user management systems that support both RBAC and ABAC, allowing organizations to take advantage of both models as needed.

Policy Management: Use policy management tools to streamline the creation, modification, and evaluation of access control policies. Consider adopting a centralized policy store to manage policies efficiently.

Logging and Monitoring: Implement robust logging and monitoring mechanisms to track access attempts and evaluate the effectiveness of access control policies. This data can inform policy adjustments and improve security.

Testing and Auditing: Regularly test and audit access control mechanisms to ensure they are functioning as intended and to identify potential vulnerabilities.

Implementing strong access control mechanisms such as Role-Based Access Control (RBAC) and Attribute-Based Access Control (ABAC) is crucial for maintaining security and protecting sensitive data within applications. While RBAC offers a straightforward approach based on user roles, ABAC provides the flexibility to incorporate dynamic attributes into access decisions. Understanding the strengths and limitations of each model allows organizations to select the appropriate access control strategy that aligns with their security requirements and operational needs. By carefully designing and managing access control policies, organizations can effectively safeguard their resources while enabling authorized users to perform their tasks efficiently.

4.3 Session Management and Preventing Session Hijacking

Effective session management is critical to ensuring the security and integrity of user sessions in web applications. When users authenticate themselves, a session is established, allowing them to interact with the application without needing to re-enter their credentials for each request. However, if not managed properly, sessions can become vulnerable to attacks such as session hijacking, where an unauthorized party takes control of an active session. This section discusses best practices for session management and strategies to prevent session hijacking.

1. Understanding Sessions

What is a Session?

A session is a temporary and interactive information interchange between two or more communicating devices, or between a user and a web application. When a user logs into an application, the server creates a session to store information about the user and their interactions with the application.

Session Lifecycle:

The session lifecycle generally involves the following steps:

- **Session Creation**: Initiated when a user successfully logs in. The server creates a unique session identifier (session ID) and stores it in the server-side session storage.
- **Session Maintenance**: The session remains active as the user interacts with the application. The server periodically checks the session ID for validation.
- **Session Termination**: The session can end when the user logs out or after a defined period of inactivity, at which point the session ID is invalidated.

2. Best Practices for Secure Session Management

1. Use Secure Session Identifiers:

Random and Unpredictable IDs: Generate session IDs using a cryptographically secure random number generator to ensure they are unique and unpredictable. Avoid using sequential numbers or any identifiable patterns that can be guessed.

Use Long Session IDs: Longer session IDs increase the complexity for attackers attempting to guess them. A session ID should ideally be at least 128 bits.

2. Secure Transmission of Session IDs:

Use HTTPS: Always transmit session IDs over secure connections (HTTPS) to prevent eavesdropping and man-in-the-middle attacks. HTTP is susceptible to interception, allowing attackers to steal session IDs.

Secure Cookies: Set the Secure and HttpOnly flags on cookies containing session IDs. The Secure flag ensures cookies are sent only over HTTPS, while HttpOnly prevents JavaScript from accessing the cookie, mitigating XSS attacks.

3. Session Timeouts:

Implement Idle Timeouts: Define a maximum idle time for user sessions. If a user is inactive for a specified period, automatically log them out and invalidate the session.

Set Maximum Session Lifetimes: Establish a maximum duration for any session, regardless of activity. Users should be required to re-authenticate after this period, further reducing the risk of unauthorized access.

4. Session Revocation:

Allow Manual Session Logout: Provide users with the option to manually log out, which should invalidate the session on the server-side immediately.

Handle Account Changes: Invalidate existing sessions when critical account changes occur, such as password updates, which can help prevent unauthorized access if a session was hijacked.

3. Preventing Session Hijacking

1. Session Hijacking Overview:

Session hijacking occurs when an attacker takes over a valid session by obtaining the session ID through various means, such as network sniffing, XSS attacks, or social engineering. Once an attacker has the session ID, they can impersonate the legitimate user.

2. Mitigation Strategies:

Session Binding:

IP Address Binding: Bind sessions to the user's IP address during their session. If the session ID is used from a different IP address, invalidate the session. However, be cautious with mobile users or users behind NAT, as their IP addresses may change.

User Agent Binding: Bind sessions to the user's browser user agent string. If a session is accessed from a different user agent, invalidate the session. This can help detect and block potential hijacking attempts.

Implement CSRF Tokens:

Cross-Site Request Forgery (CSRF) tokens are unique, unpredictable tokens that are generated for each user session. Including a CSRF token in forms and requests helps ensure that requests are made by authenticated users and not by malicious scripts.

Monitor and Log Session Activity:

Track Login Locations: Maintain logs of user login locations and activity. Notify users of suspicious login attempts and allow them to secure their accounts.

Detect Anomalies: Implement anomaly detection mechanisms that monitor for unusual session behavior, such as rapid access from different locations or devices.

Educate Users:

Awareness of Phishing Attacks: Educate users on recognizing phishing attempts and the importance of logging out from shared or public computers.

Encouraging Strong Authentication Practices: Recommend using strong passwords and enabling multi-factor authentication (MFA) to add an additional layer of security.

Effective session management is crucial for securing user interactions with web applications. By implementing best practices for session management and employing strategies to prevent session hijacking, developers can significantly enhance the security posture of their applications. Secure session identifiers, proper transmission methods, session timeouts, and robust monitoring practices all play an essential role in protecting user sessions from unauthorized access. Ultimately, a proactive approach to session management and awareness of potential threats will help safeguard sensitive data and maintain user trust in the application.

5. Data Encryption and Storage Security

In Data Encryption and Storage Security, we focus on the vital role of encryption in protecting sensitive information both at rest and in transit. This chapter covers the fundamentals of cryptographic techniques, including symmetric and asymmetric encryption, and provides guidance on selecting appropriate algorithms and libraries to ensure data confidentiality. We also explore best practices for securely storing sensitive information, such as hashing and salting passwords, and discuss effective key management strategies. By implementing robust encryption and storage security measures, developers can mitigate risks associated with data breaches and unauthorized access, safeguarding user information and maintaining compliance with regulatory requirements.

5.1 Choosing the Right Cryptographic Algorithms and Libraries

Cryptography is a cornerstone of modern security practices, providing essential mechanisms for protecting sensitive information, ensuring data integrity, and establishing secure communications. As developers design applications that rely on cryptographic methods, selecting the appropriate algorithms and libraries is crucial for ensuring robust security. This section explores the fundamental aspects of choosing the right cryptographic algorithms and libraries, highlighting key considerations, common algorithms, and best practices.

1. Understanding Cryptography Basics

What is Cryptography?

Cryptography is the science of encoding and decoding information to protect it from unauthorized access. It encompasses various techniques, including encryption, hashing, and digital signatures, each serving a specific purpose in securing data.

Key Concepts:

- **Encryption**: The process of converting plaintext into ciphertext using an algorithm and a key. Only authorized parties with the appropriate key can decrypt the ciphertext back into plaintext.

- **Hashing**: A one-way process that transforms data into a fixed-length string (hash) that represents the original data. Hashes are primarily used for data integrity verification.
- **Digital Signatures**: A cryptographic technique that allows an entity to sign a message, providing authenticity and non-repudiation. Recipients can verify the signature using the signer's public key.

2. Key Considerations for Choosing Cryptographic Algorithms

1. Purpose and Requirements:

Before selecting a cryptographic algorithm, it is essential to define the specific purpose and requirements of the application:

- **Data Confidentiality**: If the goal is to protect sensitive data from unauthorized access, symmetric or asymmetric encryption algorithms may be needed.
- **Data Integrity**: For ensuring data has not been altered, hashing algorithms are appropriate.
- **Authentication**: To verify the identity of users or systems, digital signatures and secure key exchange protocols are essential.

2. Strength and Security:

When evaluating cryptographic algorithms, consider their strength and resistance to known attacks:

- **Key Length**: Longer keys generally provide stronger security. For symmetric algorithms, keys of at least 128 bits are recommended, while for asymmetric algorithms, key lengths should be at least 2048 bits.
- **Algorithm Selection**: Favor widely accepted and vetted algorithms. Avoid using proprietary or obscure algorithms unless thoroughly reviewed by the cryptographic community.

3. Performance:

Performance considerations can influence the choice of algorithms, especially in resource-constrained environments:

- **Speed**: Symmetric algorithms (e.g., AES) are typically faster than asymmetric algorithms (e.g., RSA), making them preferable for encrypting large amounts of data.
- **Resource Usage**: Evaluate the computational overhead associated with specific algorithms and libraries. Algorithms with lower resource consumption are preferable for applications with limited processing power or memory.

4. Standards and Compliance:

Adhering to established cryptographic standards can ensure interoperability and compliance with regulations:

- **Industry Standards**: Utilize algorithms endorsed by reputable organizations such as the National Institute of Standards and Technology (NIST) or the Internet Engineering Task Force (IETF).
- **Compliance Requirements**: Ensure that the chosen algorithms meet the necessary regulatory requirements, such as GDPR, HIPAA, or PCI-DSS.

3. Common Cryptographic Algorithms

1. Symmetric Encryption Algorithms:

These algorithms use the same key for both encryption and decryption. Common symmetric algorithms include:

- **AES (Advanced Encryption Standard):** A widely used symmetric encryption standard that supports key sizes of 128, 192, and 256 bits. AES is known for its speed and security.
- **ChaCha20**: A stream cipher that provides high performance on both hardware and software implementations, often used in mobile applications.

2. Asymmetric Encryption Algorithms:

These algorithms use a pair of keys (public and private) for encryption and decryption. Common asymmetric algorithms include:

- **RSA (Rivest-Shamir-Adleman):** One of the first public-key cryptosystems, widely used for secure data transmission and digital signatures. RSA typically requires larger keys (2048 bits or more) for adequate security.

- **ECDSA (Elliptic Curve Digital Signature Algorithm):** An asymmetric algorithm that uses elliptic curves to provide strong security with smaller key sizes, making it efficient for mobile and IoT applications.

3. Hashing Algorithms:

These algorithms produce a fixed-length hash value from input data, ensuring data integrity. Common hashing algorithms include:

- **SHA-256 (Secure Hash Algorithm 256-bit):** Part of the SHA-2 family, widely used for hashing and data integrity checks.
- **bcrypt:** A hashing algorithm specifically designed for securely hashing passwords, incorporating a work factor to slow down brute-force attacks.

4. Digital Signature Algorithms:

Digital signatures ensure the authenticity and integrity of messages. Common digital signature algorithms include:

- **RSA:** Often used for signing messages and verifying the signature using the corresponding public key.
- **ECDSA:** Provides strong digital signatures with shorter keys, making it efficient for various applications.

4. Selecting Cryptographic Libraries

1. Established Libraries:

Utilize well-known and widely adopted cryptographic libraries that have undergone extensive scrutiny and peer review. Examples include:

- **OpenSSL:** A robust library that implements various cryptographic algorithms and protocols, widely used in web servers and applications.
- **Libsodium:** A modern library that offers high-level cryptographic primitives and is designed to be easy to use while ensuring security.
- **Bouncy Castle:** A comprehensive cryptographic library for Java and C#, providing a wide range of algorithms and functionalities.

2. Security Audits:

Ensure the libraries chosen have been audited and vetted by independent security experts. Libraries that have undergone public scrutiny are more likely to be secure.

3. Active Maintenance:

Choose libraries that are actively maintained and regularly updated to address vulnerabilities and improve performance. Regular updates are crucial for adapting to evolving security threats.

4. Language Compatibility:

Select libraries that are compatible with the programming languages and frameworks being used in the application to ensure seamless integration.

5. Best Practices for Cryptographic Implementation

1. Use Libraries Instead of Implementing Algorithms:

Avoid implementing cryptographic algorithms from scratch. Instead, leverage well-tested libraries to minimize the risk of introducing vulnerabilities.

2. Stay Updated on Cryptographic Developments:

Cryptography is a rapidly evolving field. Stay informed about the latest developments, emerging algorithms, and vulnerabilities in existing algorithms to ensure continued security.

3. Regularly Review and Update:

Periodically review cryptographic implementations and update algorithms and libraries as needed to address emerging threats and vulnerabilities.

Choosing the right cryptographic algorithms and libraries is vital for the security of any software application. By understanding the fundamental concepts of cryptography, evaluating algorithms based on purpose, strength, performance, and compliance, and selecting established libraries, developers can significantly enhance their applications' security posture. Following best practices for cryptographic implementation ensures that sensitive data remains protected against unauthorized access and tampering, establishing a foundation of trust with users. In an era where data breaches and cyber threats are increasingly common, implementing robust cryptographic measures is not just a best practice; it is an essential requirement for secure software development.

5.2 Storing Sensitive Data: Hashing, Salting, and Key Management

Storing sensitive data securely is crucial for protecting user information and maintaining the integrity of software applications. This section explores best practices for storing sensitive data, focusing on hashing and salting techniques for passwords, as well as effective key management strategies for encryption keys and sensitive information.

1. Understanding Sensitive Data

What is Sensitive Data?

Sensitive data includes any information that, if disclosed or compromised, could lead to identity theft, financial loss, or violation of privacy rights. Common examples include:

- Passwords
- Personal Identification Numbers (PINs)
- Social Security Numbers (SSNs)
- Credit card information
- Health records

Why Secure Sensitive Data?

Organizations are legally and ethically obligated to protect sensitive data to prevent data breaches and comply with regulations like GDPR, HIPAA, and PCI-DSS. Inadequate protection can result in significant financial penalties, reputational damage, and loss of customer trust.

2. Hashing Sensitive Data

What is Hashing?

Hashing is a one-way cryptographic function that transforms input data into a fixed-length hash value. Hash functions are designed to be irreversible, meaning that the original input cannot be easily recovered from the hash.

Characteristics of a Good Hash Function:

- **Deterministic**: The same input will always produce the same hash output.
- **Fast Computation**: The hash function should be efficient and quick to compute.
- **Pre-image Resistance**: It should be computationally infeasible to reverse the process, meaning deriving the original input from its hash is extremely difficult.
- **Collision Resistance**: It should be infeasible to find two different inputs that produce the same hash output.

Common Hashing Algorithms:

- **SHA-256**: Part of the SHA-2 family, SHA-256 generates a 256-bit hash and is widely used for data integrity checks and password storage.
- **bcrypt**: Specifically designed for securely hashing passwords, bcrypt incorporates a work factor that increases the time required to compute the hash, making it resistant to brute-force attacks.
- **Argon2**: The winner of the Password Hashing Competition, Argon2 is designed to resist both GPU and ASIC attacks and is highly configurable in terms of memory and time requirements.

3. Salting Hashes

What is Salting?

Salting is the practice of adding a unique, random value (the salt) to the input data before hashing. This ensures that even if two users have the same password, their hashes will be different, thereby mitigating the risk of rainbow table attacks.

Why Use Salts?:

- **Prevent Pre-computed Attacks**: Salting makes pre-computed attacks (e.g., rainbow tables) ineffective since the salt alters the hash output.
- **Unique Hashes**: Even identical passwords will result in different hash outputs due to the unique salts, making it much harder for attackers to use common passwords against multiple accounts.

Best Practices for Salting:

- **Unique Salts**: Generate a unique salt for each password. This can be accomplished using a secure random number generator.
- **Sufficient Length**: Use salts that are long enough (e.g., 16 bytes or more) to ensure they are unique and unpredictable.
- **Store Salts Securely**: Salts should be stored alongside the hashed passwords in the database, as they are not secret but are essential for verifying the password during authentication.

Example of Hashing with Salting:

password = "mySecurePassword"
salt = GenerateRandomSalt() // e.g., 16 bytes
hash = HashFunction(salt + password) // e.g., SHA-256 or bcrypt
StoreInDatabase(user_id, salt, hash)

4. Key Management

What is Key Management?

Key management involves the generation, distribution, storage, and destruction of cryptographic keys used for encrypting and decrypting sensitive data. Effective key management practices are essential for maintaining the security of encrypted information.

Key Management Best Practices:

1. Key Generation:

- Use a secure random number generator to create keys with sufficient entropy.
- Ensure keys are of appropriate length based on the encryption algorithm (e.g., AES-256 requires 256-bit keys).

2. Key Storage:

- **Secure Storage**: Store keys in a secure location, such as a hardware security module (HSM) or a secure key vault.
- **Access Control**: Implement strict access controls to limit who can access cryptographic keys. Only authorized personnel and applications should have access to keys.

3. Key Rotation:

- Regularly rotate encryption keys to limit the impact of a potential key compromise.
- Implement processes to re-encrypt sensitive data with new keys while ensuring old keys are securely destroyed.

4. Key Destruction:

- Securely destroy keys that are no longer needed to prevent unauthorized recovery.
- Use methods like zeroizing (overwriting with zeros) or cryptographic erasure to ensure keys cannot be recovered.

5. Audit and Monitoring:

- Maintain logs of key usage and access to detect any unauthorized attempts to access or use keys.
- Conduct regular audits of key management practices to ensure compliance with policies and standards.

5. Example of Storing Sensitive Data

Let's consider an example of storing user passwords securely using hashing, salting, and proper key management:

User Registration:

- User provides a password.
- Generate a unique salt for the user.
- Hash the password with the salt using bcrypt.
- Store the hashed password and salt in the database.

User Login:

- User submits their password.
- Retrieve the stored salt and hash from the database.
- Hash the submitted password with the retrieved salt.
- Compare the newly computed hash with the stored hash. If they match, grant access.

Storing sensitive data securely requires careful consideration of hashing, salting, and key management practices. Hashing passwords with unique salts protects against common attacks, while effective key management ensures that encryption keys remain secure and properly handled. By implementing these best practices, developers can significantly reduce the risk of data breaches and unauthorized access to sensitive information. In an era where data protection is paramount, taking the necessary steps to secure sensitive data is not just a best practice; it is an ethical obligation and a vital component of secure software development.

5.3 Encrypting Data in Transit vs. Data at Rest

Encryption is a fundamental practice in securing sensitive information, and it can be applied in two main contexts: data in transit and data at rest. Each context presents unique challenges and requirements, necessitating tailored encryption strategies. This section explores the differences between encrypting data in transit and data at rest, the associated risks, and best practices for implementing effective encryption mechanisms.

1. Understanding Data in Transit and Data at Rest

Data in Transit:

Data in transit refers to information actively moving from one location to another, whether across the internet or through private networks. This includes data sent over protocols like HTTP, HTTPS, FTP, and email transmissions. The primary concern with data in transit is its vulnerability to interception, eavesdropping, and tampering.

Data at Rest:

Data at rest refers to inactive data stored on a physical medium, such as databases, file systems, or cloud storage. This data is not actively being transmitted but is still susceptible to unauthorized access, breaches, and data theft. Common examples of data at rest include files on hard drives, databases, and backup systems.

2. Risks Associated with Data in Transit and Data at Rest

Data in Transit Risks:

- **Eavesdropping**: Attackers can intercept unencrypted data being transmitted over the network, gaining access to sensitive information such as login credentials, personal data, or financial information.

- **Man-in-the-Middle Attacks**: An attacker can intercept and alter communication between two parties, potentially injecting malicious content or capturing sensitive information.
- **Session Hijacking**: Unauthorized access to a user's session can occur if session tokens or cookies are not properly protected during transmission.

Data at Rest Risks:

- **Unauthorized Access**: Attackers gaining access to storage systems (e.g., databases, file servers) can retrieve sensitive data if it is not encrypted.
- **Data Breaches**: If a system is compromised, unencrypted data can be exfiltrated, leading to significant financial and reputational damage.
- **Physical Theft**: Lost or stolen devices (e.g., laptops, USB drives) containing sensitive data can result in data exposure if encryption is not applied.

3. Encryption for Data in Transit

1. **Purpose of Encryption in Transit**: The primary goal of encrypting data in transit is to protect it from interception and tampering while it travels across networks. Encryption ensures confidentiality, integrity, and authenticity.

2. **Common Protocols:**

- **TLS (Transport Layer Security):** The most widely used protocol for securing data in transit, TLS encrypts data sent over the internet, ensuring confidentiality and integrity. It is used in HTTPS for secure web traffic and can also secure other protocols like FTP and SMTP.
- **VPN (Virtual Private Network):** VPNs create secure tunnels for data transmission, encrypting the traffic between the user's device and the destination server, thus protecting it from eavesdropping.

3. **Best Practices for Encrypting Data in Transit:**

- **Always Use HTTPS**: Ensure that all web applications use HTTPS to encrypt data sent between the client and server.
- **Implement Strong Cipher Suites**: Use strong encryption algorithms and cipher suites for TLS, avoiding outdated protocols like SSL and weak ciphers (e.g., RC4).
- **Validate Certificates**: Always validate server certificates to prevent man-in-the-middle attacks.

- **Secure API Communications**: Use HTTPS for APIs and ensure proper authentication mechanisms are in place to protect data in transit.

4. Encryption for Data at Rest

1. **Purpose of Encryption at Rest**: The primary goal of encrypting data at rest is to protect stored data from unauthorized access and data breaches. It ensures that even if an attacker gains physical access to the storage medium, they cannot access the data without the appropriate decryption keys.

2. **Common Methods:**

- **Full Disk Encryption (FDE):** Encrypts all data on a storage device, including operating system files, applications, and user data. FDE protects data if the device is lost or stolen.
- **File-Level Encryption**: Encrypts individual files or directories, allowing for more granular control over what data is encrypted. This is useful for securing sensitive files while leaving others unencrypted.
- **Database Encryption**: Encrypts data stored in databases, ensuring that sensitive information is protected even if the database is compromised.

3. **Best Practices for Encrypting Data at Rest:**

- **Use Strong Encryption Standards**: Implement strong encryption algorithms such as AES-256 for encrypting data at rest, ensuring that keys are also managed securely.
- **Key Management**: Use a robust key management strategy to generate, store, and rotate encryption keys. Ensure that keys are stored securely and are not embedded within the encrypted data.
- **Access Controls**: Implement strict access controls to limit who can access encrypted data. Use role-based access control (RBAC) to enforce the principle of least privilege.
- **Regular Audits and Compliance Checks**: Regularly audit encryption practices and ensure compliance with relevant regulations and standards (e.g., GDPR, HIPAA).

Understanding the differences between encrypting data in transit and data at rest is essential for implementing effective security measures. Both forms of encryption play vital roles in protecting sensitive information from unauthorized access and attacks. While data in transit focuses on securing information during transmission to prevent interception, data at rest encryption ensures stored information remains protected against unauthorized access. By following best practices for both contexts, organizations can establish a comprehensive security strategy that safeguards sensitive data throughout its lifecycle. In today's data-driven world, robust encryption practices are not just recommended; they are essential for protecting user privacy and maintaining the trust of customers.

6. Securing Web Applications

In Securing Web Applications, we address the unique security challenges faced by web developers in today's threat landscape. This chapter highlights common vulnerabilities, such as cross-site scripting (XSS), cross-site request forgery (CSRF), and SQL injection, and provides practical strategies for mitigating these risks. We emphasize the importance of input validation and output encoding to prevent unauthorized data manipulation, as well as the implementation of security headers and cookie settings to enhance browser security. By adopting a proactive approach to web application security, developers can significantly reduce their exposure to attacks, ensuring that their applications are safe, reliable, and trusted by users.

6.1 Common Web Vulnerabilities and How to Mitigate Them (XSS, CSRF)

Web applications are integral to modern business operations, but they are also prime targets for various security threats. Understanding common web vulnerabilities and their mitigation strategies is essential for developers, as it allows them to build more secure applications. This section focuses on two prevalent web vulnerabilities: Cross-Site Scripting (XSS) and Cross-Site Request Forgery (CSRF), detailing their nature, impact, and mitigation techniques.

1. Understanding Cross-Site Scripting (XSS)

What is XSS?

Cross-Site Scripting (XSS) is a vulnerability that allows attackers to inject malicious scripts into web pages viewed by other users. These scripts execute in the context of the victim's browser, potentially compromising user data, session cookies, and other sensitive information.

Types of XSS:

- **Stored XSS**: Malicious scripts are permanently stored on the target server (e.g., in a database) and are served to users who visit the affected page.

- **Reflected XSS**: The malicious script is reflected off a web server, typically via a URL or an HTTP request, and executed immediately upon a user clicking a link or submitting a form.
- **DOM-based XSS**: This occurs when the vulnerability is exploited through client-side scripts. The script modifies the DOM (Document Object Model) without the server being involved.

Impact of XSS:

- **Data Theft**: Attackers can capture sensitive information such as cookies, session tokens, and user credentials.
- **Session Hijacking**: Compromised sessions can lead to unauthorized actions on behalf of the victim.
- **Defacement**: Malicious scripts can alter the appearance of web pages, damaging the website's credibility.

2. Mitigating XSS Vulnerabilities

1. Input Validation and Output Encoding:

- **Validate Input**: Always validate and sanitize user inputs on the server side to ensure that they conform to expected formats. Reject any input that does not meet the criteria.
- **Output Encoding**: Encode data before rendering it on web pages. For example, convert characters like <, >, and & into their HTML entity equivalents (<, >, &). This prevents the browser from interpreting them as executable HTML or JavaScript.

2. Use Content Security Policy (CSP):

Implement CSP headers to define which resources are allowed to be loaded on the page. This reduces the risk of XSS by preventing the execution of unauthorized scripts.

3. HttpOnly and Secure Flags on Cookies:

Set the HttpOnly flag on cookies to prevent JavaScript from accessing them, and the Secure flag to ensure cookies are only transmitted over HTTPS connections.

4. Framework-Specific Protection:

Utilize web frameworks that have built-in protections against XSS. For instance, modern frameworks like React, Angular, and Django automatically handle output encoding, reducing the likelihood of XSS vulnerabilities.

3. Understanding Cross-Site Request Forgery (CSRF)

What is CSRF?

Cross-Site Request Forgery (CSRF) is an attack that tricks a user into executing unwanted actions on a web application in which they are authenticated. This can happen when a user is logged into a web application and unknowingly submits a request to perform an action (like changing account settings) by clicking on a malicious link or loading a malicious web page.

Impact of CSRF:

- **Unauthorized Actions**: Attackers can perform actions on behalf of authenticated users without their consent, such as transferring funds, changing passwords, or altering email addresses.
- **Data Breach**: CSRF attacks can lead to exposure of sensitive information if the action performed reveals user data.

4. Mitigating CSRF Vulnerabilities

1. Use Anti-CSRF Tokens:

Generate unique tokens for each user session and include them in forms and AJAX requests. The server must validate these tokens upon receiving requests to ensure they are legitimate. If the token is missing or invalid, the server should reject the request.

2. SameSite Cookie Attribute:

Use the SameSite attribute for cookies, which restricts how cookies are sent with cross-site requests. This can prevent browsers from including cookies in requests initiated from other sites.

3. Validate HTTP Referer Header:

Check the Referer header in requests to ensure they originate from trusted sources. While this method is not foolproof (since headers can be spoofed), it adds an additional layer of protection.

4. Log Out Inactive Sessions:

Implement automatic logout after a period of inactivity to limit the window during which an attacker can exploit an active session.

Cross-Site Scripting (XSS) and Cross-Site Request Forgery (CSRF) are two significant vulnerabilities that can severely compromise the security of web applications. Understanding how these attacks work and their potential impacts is crucial for developers aiming to build secure applications. By implementing robust input validation, output encoding, anti-CSRF tokens, and employing secure cookie practices, developers can effectively mitigate these vulnerabilities. Security should be an integral part of the software development process, ensuring that user data remains protected against evolving threats. Adopting a proactive security posture not only helps safeguard applications but also fosters user trust and enhances the overall integrity of web services.

6.2 Input Validation and Output Encoding Techniques

In the realm of web application security, input validation and output encoding are critical practices to prevent various vulnerabilities, including Cross-Site Scripting (XSS) and SQL Injection. By ensuring that data entering the application is valid and properly formatted, and that data leaving the application is safe to display, developers can significantly reduce the attack surface. This section delves into effective techniques for input validation and output encoding.

1. Understanding Input Validation

What is Input Validation?

Input validation is the process of verifying that the data provided by users meets predefined criteria before it is processed by the application. The goal is to ensure that only legitimate, expected data is accepted, thereby minimizing the risk of malicious input that can lead to security vulnerabilities.

Why is Input Validation Important?

Proper input validation helps protect against various attacks, such as:

- **SQL Injection**: Attackers can manipulate SQL queries by injecting malicious input.
- **XSS**: Malicious scripts can be executed in the context of another user's browser if unvalidated input is reflected back on web pages.
- **Command Injection**: Malicious input can execute unintended commands on the server.

2. Input Validation Techniques

1. Whitelisting vs. Blacklisting:

- **Whitelisting**: Accept only known good values. For instance, if an input field only allows numbers, specify that only numeric input is valid. This is the most secure approach.
- **Blacklisting**: Reject known bad values. However, this approach is less effective because attackers can find ways to bypass the blacklist.

2. Type Checking:

Ensure that the input matches the expected data type. For example, if an integer is expected, verify that the input is indeed an integer and not a string or other type.

3. Length Checking:

Enforce length restrictions on input data. For example, restrict usernames to a maximum of 20 characters to prevent buffer overflow attacks.

4. Format Validation:

Validate input against specific formats using regular expressions. For example, ensure that email addresses conform to a standard pattern (^[\w-\.]+@([\w-]+\.)+[\w-]{2,4}$).

5. Sanitization:

Remove or neutralize dangerous characters from input. This is particularly important when dealing with inputs that may be included in SQL queries or HTML output.

6. Contextual Validation:

Validate input based on its context within the application. For example, an input value may be valid in one context (e.g., an order quantity) but invalid in another (e.g., a username).

3. Understanding Output Encoding

What is Output Encoding?

Output encoding is the practice of converting data into a format that is safe for output in a specific context (e.g., HTML, JavaScript, URL). This is crucial for preventing XSS and ensuring that data displayed to users cannot be executed as code.

Why is Output Encoding Important?

Output encoding mitigates the risk of XSS by ensuring that any potentially harmful data is treated as plain text rather than executable code. This means that even if an attacker succeeds in injecting malicious scripts, those scripts will not be executed in the user's browser.

4. Output Encoding Techniques

1. HTML Encoding:

Encode characters to their HTML entity equivalents to prevent browsers from interpreting them as HTML. For example:

< becomes <
> becomes >
& becomes &

2. JavaScript Encoding:

When including user input in JavaScript, encode special characters to prevent execution. For example, use escape() or encodeURIComponent() functions.

3. URL Encoding:

When data is included in URLs, encode special characters to ensure they are treated as data rather than control characters. For instance, space becomes %20.

4. Attribute Encoding:

When outputting data within HTML attributes, ensure that values are properly encoded to prevent XSS. For instance, within an href attribute, encode the URL.

5. Use Framework Libraries:

Utilize built-in encoding functions provided by web frameworks. Most modern frameworks (e.g., React, Angular, Django) offer automatic output encoding to mitigate XSS risks effectively.

5. Best Practices for Input Validation and Output Encoding

Always Validate Input: No matter the source, always validate and sanitize input data. Never trust data coming from users, as it can be malicious.

Use Secure Coding Practices: Follow secure coding guidelines and leverage frameworks that provide built-in security features.

Keep Libraries Up-to-Date: Ensure that third-party libraries are up to date with the latest security patches to mitigate known vulnerabilities.

Test for Vulnerabilities: Regularly test applications for input validation and output encoding vulnerabilities using security tools and manual testing.

Educate Developers: Provide training for developers on secure coding practices, including input validation and output encoding.

Input validation and output encoding are fundamental practices in securing web applications. By properly validating input data and encoding output, developers can significantly reduce the risk of vulnerabilities such as XSS and SQL Injection. Implementing these techniques not only protects sensitive data but also enhances the overall security posture of the application. As the threat landscape continues to evolve, incorporating robust validation and encoding practices into the software development lifecycle is essential for maintaining user trust and safeguarding information in the digital age.

6.3 Implementing Security Headers and Cookie Security

In an era where web applications are increasingly targeted by cyber threats, securing user data and maintaining the integrity of applications is paramount. One effective way to enhance the security posture of web applications is through the implementation of security headers and robust cookie security practices. This section delves into the significance of security headers, the specific headers that should be implemented, and best practices for ensuring cookie security.

1. Understanding Security Headers

What are Security Headers?

Security headers are HTTP response headers that help protect web applications from various attacks by instructing the browser on how to handle certain content and behavior. By configuring security headers properly, developers can mitigate risks such as Cross-Site Scripting (XSS), Clickjacking, and other attacks.

Why are Security Headers Important?

Security headers provide an additional layer of defense by enabling browsers to enforce certain security policies. They help prevent a range of attacks and ensure that users interact with the application in a safe and secure environment.

2. Essential Security Headers to Implement

1. Content Security Policy (CSP):

Description: CSP is a powerful security feature that helps prevent XSS attacks by specifying which sources of content are considered trustworthy.

Implementation: A typical CSP header might look like this:

Content-Security-Policy: default-src 'self'; script-src 'self' https://trusted.cdn.com; object-src 'none';

Best Practices: Start with a restrictive policy and gradually loosen it as necessary. Use the report-uri directive to collect CSP violation reports for monitoring.

2. X-Content-Type-Options:

Description: This header prevents browsers from interpreting files as a different MIME type than what is specified. It helps prevent attacks where content is served with a misleading MIME type.

Implementation: Use the following header:

X-Content-Type-Options: nosniff

3. X-Frame-Options:

Description: This header helps prevent Clickjacking by controlling whether a page can be displayed in a frame or iframe.

Implementation: Common values include DENY (disallow framing) and SAMEORIGIN (allow framing only from the same origin):

X-Frame-Options: DENY

4. X-XSS-Protection:

Description: This header enables the cross-site scripting filter built into most modern browsers.

Implementation: Use the following header to enable it:

X-XSS-Protection: 1; mode=block

5. Strict-Transport-Security (HSTS):

Description: HSTS instructs browsers to only interact with the server over HTTPS, protecting against man-in-the-middle attacks.

Implementation: The header should be configured as follows:

Strict-Transport-Security: max-age=31536000; includeSubDomains

6. Referrer-Policy:

Description: This header controls how much referrer information should be passed when navigating away from a page.

Implementation: A common setting is:

Referrer-Policy: no-referrer

3. Implementing Cookie Security

Cookies are a fundamental part of web applications, used for session management and storing user preferences. However, they can also be exploited if not configured securely. Implementing cookie security is essential to protect user data.

1. Secure Flag:

Description: This flag ensures that cookies are only sent over HTTPS connections. It prevents the cookie from being transmitted in plaintext over unsecured connections.

Implementation: Set the secure flag in your cookie configuration:

Set-Cookie: sessionId=abc123; Secure

2. HttpOnly Flag:

Description: This flag prevents client-side scripts from accessing the cookie, mitigating the risk of XSS attacks stealing session cookies.

Implementation: Set the HttpOnly flag in your cookie configuration:

Set-Cookie: sessionId=abc123; HttpOnly

3. SameSite Attribute:

Description: The SameSite attribute controls whether cookies are sent with cross-origin requests, reducing the risk of CSRF attacks.

Implementation: The SameSite attribute can take values such as Strict, Lax, or None. For example:

Set-Cookie: sessionId=abc123; SameSite=Lax

4. Expiration and Max-Age:

Description: Setting an appropriate expiration date or max-age for cookies can help limit the window of opportunity for attackers if a session is compromised.

Implementation: Example of setting a max-age:

Set-Cookie: sessionId=abc123; Max-Age=3600 # Expires in one hour

5. Avoiding Storing Sensitive Information:

Description: Avoid storing sensitive information (like passwords or credit card details) directly in cookies. Use secure server-side storage and reference session identifiers in cookies instead.

4. Best Practices for Security Headers and Cookie Security

Review and Test Security Configurations: Regularly review and test the implementation of security headers and cookie settings to ensure they are correctly applied and functioning as intended.

Monitor Security Reports: Use CSP reports to monitor for violations and adjust your policy as needed. Tools and services can help visualize and analyze these reports.

Combine Security Measures: Utilize multiple layers of security. Relying solely on headers or cookie security is not enough; ensure that your application follows secure coding practices and conducts regular security audits.

Educate Development Teams: Provide training for development teams on the importance of security headers and cookie security practices, emphasizing their role in safeguarding user data.

Stay Updated: Security is an evolving field; stay informed about new threats and best practices. Regularly update your security measures based on current trends and vulnerabilities.

Implementing security headers and ensuring cookie security are critical components of a robust web application security strategy. By configuring essential security headers, developers can mitigate a wide range of attacks and enhance the protection of their applications. Coupled with secure cookie practices, these measures significantly reduce vulnerabilities and safeguard sensitive user data. As the threat landscape evolves, maintaining vigilance and regularly updating security practices will help organizations protect their users and maintain trust in their applications.

7. API Security and Secure Data Exchange

In API Security and Secure Data Exchange, we examine the critical role of application programming interfaces (APIs) in modern software development and the unique security challenges they present. This chapter covers essential strategies for securing APIs, including robust authentication methods, such as OAuth and API keys, and effective authorization practices to control access to sensitive data. We also discuss the importance of rate limiting and throttling to prevent abuse and denial-of-service attacks. Furthermore, we explore secure data exchange practices, emphasizing the need for HTTPS and TLS to protect data in transit. By implementing these security measures, developers can safeguard their APIs and ensure secure, reliable interactions between applications and users.

7.1 RESTful API Security: Authentication and Authorization

In the modern web ecosystem, RESTful APIs (Representational State Transfer Application Programming Interfaces) serve as crucial components that facilitate communication between clients and servers. Given their extensive use, securing RESTful APIs is paramount to safeguarding sensitive data and ensuring that only authorized users have access to specific resources. This section explores the key concepts of authentication and authorization within the context of RESTful API security, outlining best practices and strategies to mitigate potential risks.

1. Understanding Authentication and Authorization

Authentication is the process of verifying the identity of a user or system, confirming that they are who they claim to be. In the context of RESTful APIs, authentication ensures that users provide valid credentials before they can access the API.

Authorization, on the other hand, determines what an authenticated user is allowed to do. This involves granting or denying access to specific resources based on predefined roles, permissions, or policies.

2. Common Authentication Mechanisms

Several authentication mechanisms can be employed to secure RESTful APIs, each with its advantages and considerations:

1. Basic Authentication:

Description: This method involves sending a username and password encoded in Base64 with each API request in the Authorization header. For example:

Authorization: Basic dXNlcm5hbWU6cGFzc3dvcmQ=

Pros: Simple to implement; supported by most HTTP clients.

Cons: Credentials are sent with each request; requires HTTPS to secure the transmission.

2. Token-Based Authentication:

Description: Instead of sending credentials with each request, users authenticate once and receive a token (usually a JSON Web Token, or JWT). This token is then included in the Authorization header for subsequent requests:

Authorization: Bearer <token>

Pros: Stateless and scalable; tokens can be easily invalidated and renewed.

Cons: Token storage must be secure; tokens can be intercepted if not properly secured.

3. OAuth 2.0:

Description: OAuth 2.0 is a widely used framework for delegated authorization. It allows third-party applications to obtain limited access to a user's resources without sharing their credentials. This involves various grant types, including authorization code, implicit, and client credentials.

Pros: Flexible and secure; supports multiple client types (web, mobile, desktop).

Cons: Complex implementation; requires a thorough understanding of the OAuth framework.

4. OpenID Connect:

Description: Built on top of OAuth 2.0, OpenID Connect adds an identity layer, allowing clients to verify the identity of end-users based on the authentication performed by an authorization server.

Pros: Provides both authentication and authorization; widely supported by identity providers.

Cons: Requires additional setup; slightly more complex than basic OAuth.

3. Understanding Authorization Mechanisms

Once a user is authenticated, authorization ensures that they can only access resources they are permitted to. The following are common approaches to authorization in RESTful APIs:

1. Role-Based Access Control (RBAC):

Description: In RBAC, access rights are assigned based on roles within an organization. Each role has specific permissions attached, and users are granted roles that correspond to their job functions.

Pros: Simple to manage; aligns with organizational structure.

Cons: Can become cumbersome with numerous roles; inflexible to dynamic access needs.

2. Attribute-Based Access Control (ABAC):

Description: ABAC evaluates access requests based on attributes of the user, resource, and environment. Policies are defined to determine access rights dynamically based on attributes.

Pros: Flexible and fine-grained control; accommodates complex scenarios.

Cons: More complex to implement and manage; may require a dedicated policy engine.

3. Permission-Based Access Control:

Description: In this model, specific permissions are assigned to users or groups directly, allowing or denying access to resources based on those permissions.

Pros: Highly granular control over access; easy to audit permissions.

Cons: Can become complex with a large number of users and permissions.

4. Best Practices for API Authentication and Authorization

Use HTTPS: Always transmit sensitive information over HTTPS to protect credentials and tokens from interception.

Implement Token Expiration: Set expiration times for tokens to limit their validity and reduce the impact of a compromised token. Implement refresh tokens for long-lived sessions.

Secure Token Storage: Store tokens securely on the client side (e.g., in memory, local storage, or cookies with secure attributes).

Use Strong Password Policies: Enforce strong password requirements and encourage the use of multi-factor authentication (MFA) for added security.

Log and Monitor API Activity: Implement logging and monitoring to detect unusual access patterns and potential security breaches.

Regularly Review Permissions: Periodically review roles and permissions to ensure they align with current organizational needs and remove any unnecessary access.

Implement Rate Limiting and Throttling: Protect APIs from abuse by implementing rate limiting and throttling mechanisms to control the number of requests from a user or client over a given period.

Validate Input and Output: Always validate input data and sanitize output to prevent injection attacks and ensure that only safe data is processed.

Use Security Headers: Implement relevant security headers (e.g., CORS, CSP, etc.) to further protect APIs from various attacks.

Securing RESTful APIs through robust authentication and authorization mechanisms is essential for protecting sensitive data and ensuring the integrity of web applications. By leveraging secure authentication methods such as token-based authentication or OAuth 2.0, along with effective authorization strategies like RBAC and ABAC, developers can significantly enhance the security of their APIs. Coupled with best practices like HTTPS usage, secure token storage, and ongoing monitoring, organizations can build resilient APIs that safeguard user data against evolving threats. As the digital landscape continues to grow and change, implementing effective security measures is not just advisable—it's essential.

7.2 Rate Limiting and Throttling to Prevent Abuse

In the context of RESTful APIs, protecting resources from excessive use and potential abuse is crucial. Rate limiting and throttling are two effective strategies that help mitigate risks such as denial-of-service (DoS) attacks, abusive behavior, and unintentional resource exhaustion. This section explores the concepts of rate limiting and throttling, their importance, implementation strategies, and best practices to ensure robust API security.

1. Understanding Rate Limiting and Throttling

Rate Limiting is a technique that restricts the number of requests a client can make to an API within a specific timeframe. It helps control traffic and ensures that a single user or application does not overwhelm the server with too many requests.

Throttling is a broader concept that involves controlling the rate at which requests are processed, especially during peak usage times. It may involve queuing requests or temporarily blocking users when they exceed certain thresholds.

Both techniques serve to maintain the integrity and availability of the API while providing a better experience for all users.

2. Why Rate Limiting and Throttling Matter

Implementing rate limiting and throttling is vital for several reasons:

Prevent Abuse: By controlling the number of requests, APIs can defend against malicious actors attempting to overwhelm the system (e.g., DoS attacks).

Manage Server Load: During high traffic periods, these mechanisms help ensure fair usage, preventing server overload and ensuring that resources are available to all legitimate users.

Enhance User Experience: Rate limiting prevents individual users from monopolizing API resources, allowing for smoother interactions for all users.

Protect Against Exploits: By limiting the rate at which actions can be taken (like login attempts), APIs can reduce the risk of brute-force attacks.

Resource Allocation: Helps allocate server resources effectively, ensuring that more critical services are available even during peak usage.

3. Strategies for Implementing Rate Limiting

There are several approaches to implementing rate limiting, each with its advantages and considerations:

1. Token Bucket Algorithm:

Description: This algorithm allows a certain number of requests to be processed in bursts. Each client is given a "bucket" that fills with tokens at a fixed rate. Each request consumes a token. If the bucket is empty, requests are denied until tokens are available.

Pros: Allows bursts of traffic while maintaining an overall average rate. Good for scenarios with unpredictable traffic patterns.

2. Leaky Bucket Algorithm:

Description: Similar to the token bucket, but the leaky bucket enforces a steady output rate. Incoming requests are placed in a queue (the bucket), and requests are processed at a constant rate, regardless of burstiness.

Pros: Ensures a consistent flow of requests, making it ideal for preventing spikes in traffic.

3. Fixed Window Counter:

Description: This method counts the number of requests made in a fixed time window (e.g., per minute). If the limit is reached, further requests are rejected until the next time window starts.

Pros: Simple to implement and understand. Suitable for straightforward scenarios.

4. Sliding Log Window:

Description: Instead of fixed time windows, this method maintains a log of timestamps for each request. When a new request is received, it checks the log and counts how many requests were made in the defined time frame.

Pros: More precise, as it can accurately track requests in real-time. It handles bursts better than fixed window counters.

4. Strategies for Implementing Throttling

Throttling strategies focus on controlling the rate at which requests are processed, especially during peak times. Here are some common techniques:

1. Queuing Requests:

Description: When the system is under heavy load, incoming requests can be queued and processed in order. This allows the server to handle bursts of requests without crashing.

Pros: Ensures all requests are eventually processed, preventing loss of requests during peak load.

2. Backoff Strategies:

Description: When clients exceed their allowed rate, they can be instructed to back off and retry after a certain period. Exponential backoff, where the wait time increases exponentially with each retry attempt, is a common method.

Pros: Helps reduce server load by gradually reducing the number of repeated requests from clients.

3. IP-Based Throttling:

Description: Limit requests based on the IP address of the client. If a single IP exceeds the threshold, further requests from that IP are temporarily blocked or delayed.

Pros: Helps mitigate abuse from specific clients and reduces the risk of DoS attacks.

5. Best Practices for Rate Limiting and Throttling

Define Clear Policies: Establish and communicate clear rate limiting policies (e.g., requests per minute/hour) to users so they know what to expect.

Monitor API Usage: Implement monitoring and analytics to track API usage patterns. Use this data to adjust rate limits as needed.

Provide Feedback: When users hit rate limits, return appropriate HTTP status codes (e.g., 429 Too Many Requests) along with informative messages explaining the situation.

Dynamic Rate Limits: Consider implementing dynamic rate limits that adjust based on real-time server load and traffic patterns. For example, increase limits during off-peak hours and decrease during peak times.

Graceful Degradation: Implement a strategy for gracefully degrading service when limits are reached, allowing users to still access limited functionality.

Testing and Simulation: Regularly test your rate limiting and throttling mechanisms under various scenarios to ensure they work as expected and don't adversely affect legitimate users.

Documentation: Clearly document your rate limiting and throttling policies in API documentation, including how users can monitor their usage and what happens when they exceed limits.

Rate limiting and throttling are essential techniques for protecting RESTful APIs from abuse and ensuring fair resource allocation among users. By implementing effective strategies, such as the token bucket algorithm or queuing requests, organizations can maintain the integrity and availability of their services while enhancing user experience. As the digital landscape continues to evolve, understanding and applying these techniques will be critical in defending against emerging threats and ensuring a reliable API experience. By continuously monitoring usage patterns and adapting policies accordingly, developers can create resilient APIs that safeguard both their infrastructure and their users.

7.3 Securing Data in Transit with HTTPS, TLS, and API Gateways

As the volume of sensitive information exchanged over the internet continues to grow, ensuring the security of data in transit has become paramount. This section delves into the mechanisms for securing data in transit, focusing on HTTPS (Hypertext Transfer Protocol Secure), TLS (Transport Layer Security), and the role of API gateways in safeguarding communications between clients and servers.

1. Understanding Data in Transit

Data in Transit refers to information actively moving from one location to another over a network. This includes data being sent from a client to a server or between servers. Because this data traverses various networks, it is susceptible to interception and tampering by malicious actors. Therefore, protecting data in transit is critical to maintaining confidentiality, integrity, and authenticity.

2. HTTPS: The Foundation of Secure Web Communication

What is HTTPS?

HTTPS is an extension of HTTP, the protocol used for transmitting data over the web. It combines HTTP with TLS to provide a secure channel over an insecure network. When a user connects to a website using HTTPS, the data exchanged is encrypted, making it difficult for third parties to read or alter.

How HTTPS Works:

- **Encryption**: HTTPS encrypts data using TLS, ensuring that sensitive information (like passwords and personal data) is not transmitted in plaintext.
- **Authentication**: HTTPS verifies the identity of the server using SSL/TLS certificates, which are issued by trusted certificate authorities (CAs).
- **Data Integrity**: HTTPS ensures that the data sent and received is not tampered with during transmission.

Benefits of Using HTTPS:

- **Confidentiality**: Protects sensitive information from being intercepted by unauthorized parties.
- **Trust**: Users are more likely to trust websites with HTTPS, as browsers indicate a secure connection (e.g., showing a padlock icon).
- **SEO Advantage**: Search engines, such as Google, consider HTTPS as a ranking factor, providing an incentive for website owners to adopt it.

3. Transport Layer Security (TLS)

What is TLS?

TLS is a cryptographic protocol that provides end-to-end security for data in transit. It has evolved from the earlier SSL (Secure Sockets Layer) protocols and is now the standard for secure internet communication.

How TLS Works:

Handshake Process: TLS establishes a secure connection through a handshake process. During this phase, the client and server exchange cryptographic keys and agree on encryption algorithms. This involves several steps:

- The client sends a "ClientHello" message, indicating supported cipher suites and TLS versions.
- The server responds with a "ServerHello" message, selecting the cipher suite and TLS version to use.
- The server sends its digital certificate to authenticate itself.
- The client verifies the server's certificate and generates a session key for encryption.
- Both parties confirm that the handshake is complete, and secure communication begins.

Encryption Algorithms: TLS uses various algorithms, including symmetric encryption (for encrypting data), asymmetric encryption (for exchanging keys), and hashing (for ensuring data integrity).

Benefits of TLS:

- **Increased Security**: TLS provides robust encryption and is constantly updated to address vulnerabilities, making it more secure than its predecessor, SSL.
- **Wide Adoption**: TLS is widely supported across various platforms and applications, ensuring compatibility and ease of implementation.

4. Role of API Gateways in Securing Data in Transit

What is an API Gateway?

An API gateway is a server that acts as an intermediary between clients and backend services. It serves as a single entry point for API requests, managing traffic and providing various functions, including security.

Functions of API Gateways in Data Security:

Authentication and Authorization: API gateways can enforce security policies by requiring authentication and authorization for incoming requests, ensuring that only legitimate users have access to the API.

TLS Termination: An API gateway can handle TLS termination, managing the encryption and decryption of data, which offloads this processing from backend services. This can improve performance and simplify the management of SSL certificates.

Traffic Management: API gateways can implement rate limiting and throttling to prevent abuse and ensure fair usage of resources. They can also log traffic for monitoring and analysis.

Data Validation and Transformation: Gateways can validate incoming requests for structure and content before passing them to backend services. They can also transform requests and responses to ensure compatibility between clients and services.

Protection Against Attacks: API gateways can help protect against common threats like SQL injection, Cross-Site Scripting (XSS), and Distributed Denial of Service (DDoS) attacks through various security measures, such as input validation and anomaly detection.

5. Best Practices for Securing Data in Transit

Enforce HTTPS Everywhere: Always use HTTPS for all API endpoints and web pages to ensure that data is encrypted during transmission.

Use Strong TLS Configurations: Configure your server to use strong TLS settings, disabling outdated protocols (like SSL and older versions of TLS) and weak cipher suites. Utilize tools to test your TLS configuration and ensure it meets security standards.

Regularly Update Certificates: Ensure that SSL/TLS certificates are kept up to date and renew them before they expire. Use automated tools for certificate management to prevent lapses.

Implement API Gateway Security Features: Leverage the security features provided by your API gateway, such as authentication, authorization, and traffic management, to enhance the security of your APIs.

Monitor and Log Traffic: Implement logging and monitoring for all API traffic to detect anomalies and potential security breaches. Analyze logs regularly to identify suspicious patterns.

Educate Users: Educate users on the importance of secure connections and encourage them to look for indicators of security, such as the padlock icon in the browser.

Utilize HSTS (HTTP Strict Transport Security): Implement HSTS to enforce the use of HTTPS and prevent downgrade attacks by ensuring that browsers only connect to the server over secure connections.

Perform Regular Security Audits: Conduct regular security audits and vulnerability assessments of your API and its infrastructure to identify and mitigate potential risks.

Securing data in transit is a critical aspect of safeguarding sensitive information in today's digital landscape. By utilizing HTTPS and TLS, organizations can establish secure channels for communication, protecting data from interception and tampering. Moreover, API gateways play a vital role in enhancing security by managing traffic, enforcing authentication, and mitigating various threats. By following best practices and continually monitoring security measures, organizations can create resilient APIs that maintain the integrity, confidentiality, and authenticity of data as it travels across the network. As cyber threats evolve, a proactive approach to securing data in transit is essential for maintaining user trust and ensuring the safety of digital transactions.

8. Secure Software Design and Architecture

In Secure Software Design and Architecture, we explore the foundational principles that guide the creation of secure systems from the ground up. This chapter emphasizes the importance of incorporating security considerations into the design and architecture phases of software development, advocating for strategies like the principle of least privilege and the zero trust model. We delve into best practices for designing secure microservices and containerized applications, focusing on how to manage inter-service communication securely. By prioritizing security in the architectural decisions and design choices, developers can build systems that are not only resilient to attacks but also flexible and scalable, ensuring that security remains a core aspect of the application's lifecycle.

8.1 Security in Microservices and Containerized Environments

As organizations increasingly adopt microservices architectures and containerized environments, ensuring security within these frameworks has become paramount. Microservices offer modularity, flexibility, and scalability, while containers facilitate rapid deployment and resource efficiency. However, these advantages come with unique security challenges that must be addressed to protect sensitive data and maintain application integrity. This section explores the security considerations in microservices and containerized environments, key vulnerabilities, and best practices for enhancing security.

1. Understanding Microservices and Containerization

Microservices Architecture:

Microservices is an architectural style that structures an application as a collection of small, independently deployable services. Each service focuses on a specific business capability and communicates with other services through APIs. This modular approach enables organizations to scale, develop, and deploy applications more efficiently.

Containerization:

Containerization encapsulates an application and its dependencies into a lightweight, portable container that can run consistently across different environments. Docker is the most widely used containerization platform, allowing developers to create, deploy, and manage containers easily.

While microservices and containerization provide significant advantages, they also introduce complexity in security management. With multiple services and containers running in diverse environments, ensuring consistent security policies and practices becomes critical.

2. Key Security Challenges in Microservices

Increased Attack Surface:

Each microservice operates independently and communicates with other services over the network. This increases the number of potential entry points for attackers, expanding the attack surface.

Service-to-Service Communication:

In microservices architectures, services must communicate securely. If these communications are not properly secured, they can be intercepted or manipulated by malicious actors.

Identity and Access Management:

Managing user identities and service identities across multiple microservices can be challenging. Ensuring proper authentication and authorization mechanisms are in place is critical to preventing unauthorized access.

Data Security:

With distributed data storage across various microservices, protecting sensitive data from unauthorized access and breaches becomes complex.

Configuration Management:

Misconfigurations can lead to security vulnerabilities. Ensuring that each service and its associated containers are securely configured is essential to maintaining a secure environment.

Monitoring and Logging:

Collecting and analyzing logs from multiple services can be challenging, making it difficult to detect anomalies and respond to security incidents effectively.

3. Key Security Challenges in Containerized Environments

Container Isolation:

Containers share the same kernel, making it essential to ensure proper isolation between them. A vulnerability in one container could potentially compromise others.

Vulnerable Container Images:

Many organizations use pre-built container images from public repositories, which may contain known vulnerabilities. Regularly scanning and updating these images is crucial.

Runtime Security:

Securing containers during runtime is essential. Without proper monitoring, containers can be exploited in real time, leading to data breaches or service disruptions.

Orchestration Security:

Container orchestration platforms, like Kubernetes, manage the deployment, scaling, and operation of containers. Misconfigurations or vulnerabilities in these platforms can expose the entire container ecosystem to risks.

Supply Chain Security:

The container ecosystem relies on various components, libraries, and images. Ensuring the security of this supply chain is critical to prevent vulnerabilities from entering the environment.

4. Best Practices for Securing Microservices and Containerized Environments

Adopt a Zero Trust Model:

Implement a zero-trust security model, where all entities (services, users, and devices) are treated as untrusted by default. This requires strict verification for all communications and access attempts.

Use API Security Mechanisms:

Secure communication between microservices using robust authentication and authorization mechanisms, such as OAuth2 and JSON Web Tokens (JWT). Ensure that all API calls are encrypted using TLS.

Implement Service Mesh:

A service mesh (like Istio or Linkerd) provides advanced traffic management, security, and observability for microservices. It can handle service-to-service communication securely and efficiently.

Scan and Harden Container Images:

Regularly scan container images for vulnerabilities and ensure that only trusted images are used in production. Implement best practices for hardening container images, such as minimizing the number of packages and applying security patches promptly.

Limit Container Privileges:

Run containers with the least privilege necessary. Use non-root users and restrict capabilities to minimize the risk of exploitation.

Enforce Network Policies:

Use network policies to control traffic between microservices and containers. Ensure that only the necessary communications are allowed, reducing the risk of lateral movement in case of a breach.

Centralized Logging and Monitoring:

Implement centralized logging and monitoring solutions to collect and analyze logs from all services and containers. Utilize tools that provide real-time alerts and anomaly detection.

Regularly Audit Configurations:

Conduct regular audits of configurations for all microservices and containers. Use automated tools to detect misconfigurations and compliance violations.

Implement Secrets Management:

Use secure methods for managing sensitive data such as API keys, passwords, and tokens. Utilize secrets management solutions (e.g., HashiCorp Vault, AWS Secrets Manager) to store and access secrets securely.

Conduct Regular Security Assessments:

Perform regular security assessments, including penetration testing and vulnerability scanning, to identify and address potential security risks in microservices and containerized environments.

Securing microservices and containerized environments is a multifaceted challenge that requires a proactive and comprehensive approach. As organizations adopt these modern architectures, understanding the unique security risks and implementing best practices is critical to protecting sensitive data and maintaining application integrity. By leveraging security frameworks, adopting a zero-trust model, and employing robust monitoring and management strategies, organizations can create secure microservices architectures that effectively defend against evolving threats. As the landscape of software development continues to evolve, ongoing vigilance and adaptation are essential for maintaining security in an increasingly complex environment.

8.2 Principles of Secure Application Architecture (Least Privilege, Zero Trust)

In an era where cyber threats are more prevalent and sophisticated, secure application architecture is essential for safeguarding sensitive data and maintaining the integrity of systems. Two fundamental principles in this domain are the Least Privilege and Zero Trust models. Understanding and implementing these principles can significantly reduce the risk of unauthorized access and data breaches. This section delves into these principles, their importance, and best practices for their implementation.

1. Understanding the Least Privilege Principle

Definition:

The principle of Least Privilege (PoLP) stipulates that users, applications, and systems should have only the minimum level of access necessary to perform their legitimate functions. By restricting access rights, organizations can limit the potential damage from accidents or malicious actions.

Importance of Least Privilege:

- **Minimized Attack Surface**: By limiting access, the number of potential entry points for attackers is reduced. If a user or application is compromised, the impact is contained.
- **Reduced Risk of Data Breaches**: With less access, sensitive data is better protected from unauthorized exposure or misuse.
- **Mitigated Insider Threats**: This principle is particularly effective against insider threats, as it ensures that individuals have access only to the information and resources they need for their roles.
- **Regulatory Compliance**: Many regulations and standards, such as GDPR, HIPAA, and PCI DSS, mandate least privilege access as part of their security requirements.

Implementation of Least Privilege:

- **Role-Based Access Control (RBAC):** Define user roles and assign permissions based on the principle of least privilege. Users should be granted the minimum permissions required to perform their job functions.
- **Regular Access Reviews**: Conduct periodic audits of user access rights to ensure that permissions remain appropriate as roles and responsibilities evolve.
- **Just-in-Time Access**: Implement a just-in-time access model where users are granted temporary access to systems and data when needed, which automatically expires after use.
- **Use of Service Accounts**: For applications and services, use dedicated service accounts with limited permissions instead of using admin accounts, which can lead to unnecessary risk.
- **Segregation of Duties:** Separate critical tasks among different users to prevent any single user from having control over all aspects of a sensitive process.

2. Understanding the Zero Trust Model

Definition:

The Zero Trust model is a security framework based on the premise that no entity—whether inside or outside the network—should be trusted by default. Instead, verification is required from everyone attempting to gain access to resources on the network.

Importance of Zero Trust:

- **Mitigation of Advanced Threats**: With the rise of sophisticated cyberattacks, relying solely on perimeter defenses (like firewalls) is insufficient. Zero Trust assumes that breaches can occur and focuses on minimizing damage.
- **Protection Against Insider Threats**: Since the model does not inherently trust internal users or devices, it reduces the risk of insider threats exploiting their access rights.
- **Support for Remote Work**: As remote work becomes more common, Zero Trust allows organizations to securely extend their networks to users accessing from outside traditional office environments.
- **Comprehensive Access Controls**: Zero Trust emphasizes continuous verification and access controls, which provide enhanced security for sensitive data and systems.

Implementation of Zero Trust:

- **Identity and Access Management (IAM):** Employ robust IAM solutions to manage user identities, roles, and access permissions. Multi-factor authentication (MFA) should be enforced to strengthen identity verification.
- **Micro-Segmentation**: Divide the network into smaller segments, ensuring that access controls are enforced at the segment level. This limits lateral movement for potential attackers within the network.
- **Continuous Monitoring and Analytics**: Implement real-time monitoring and behavioral analytics to detect anomalies and potential threats. By continuously evaluating user behavior and access requests, organizations can quickly identify and respond to suspicious activity.
- **Data Encryption**: Encrypt sensitive data both at rest and in transit to protect it from unauthorized access, ensuring that even if data is intercepted, it remains unreadable.
- **Policy Enforcement**: Establish clear security policies for accessing applications and data, and ensure that these policies are enforced consistently across the organization.

3. Integrating Least Privilege and Zero Trust in Application Architecture

While Least Privilege and Zero Trust can be implemented independently, integrating these principles into an overarching security strategy enhances application security. Here's how to combine these approaches effectively:

Identity-Centric Security: Both models rely heavily on identity verification. By focusing on user identities and their access rights, organizations can enforce both least privilege and Zero Trust principles.

Contextual Access Controls: Implement access controls based on context—such as user behavior, device health, and location—to ensure that only authenticated and authorized users can access resources.

Layered Security: Utilize a defense-in-depth approach that combines multiple security layers, including network security, application security, and endpoint security, to create a more resilient architecture.

Incident Response Plans: Develop incident response plans that incorporate the lessons learned from applying least privilege and Zero Trust principles. This includes clearly defined roles and responsibilities in the event of a security incident.

Education and Training: Educate employees on the importance of these principles and how they contribute to the overall security posture. Regular training sessions can help reinforce good security practices.

Implementing the principles of Least Privilege and Zero Trust is crucial for securing modern application architectures. These principles not only protect sensitive data from unauthorized access but also mitigate the risks associated with advanced threats and insider attacks. By adopting a proactive security posture that prioritizes least privilege access and continuous verification, organizations can significantly enhance their overall security frameworks. As cyber threats continue to evolve, embracing these principles will be essential for building resilient applications that safeguard user data and maintain trust in digital interactions.

8.3 Scalability and Security Resilience in Design

As organizations grow and technology evolves, the demand for scalable and secure applications has never been more critical. In today's digital landscape, applications must be able to handle increasing loads, adapt to changing business needs, and maintain robust security against an ever-evolving threat landscape. This section explores the concepts of scalability and security resilience in application design, detailing best practices and considerations for creating systems that can effectively manage growth while ensuring strong security.

1. Understanding Scalability

Definition:

Scalability refers to the ability of an application to handle an increasing amount of work or its potential to accommodate growth. A scalable system can efficiently manage increased loads—whether through increased user traffic, more transactions, or additional features—without compromising performance.

Types of Scalability:

Vertical Scalability (Scaling Up): Involves adding resources to a single node or server, such as increasing CPU, memory, or storage. While vertical scaling can be straightforward, it has limitations in terms of maximum capacity and can lead to single points of failure.

Horizontal Scalability (Scaling Out): Involves adding more nodes or servers to the system. This approach is often more effective for handling increased loads as it distributes the workload across multiple machines, enhancing both performance and reliability.

Importance of Scalability:

- **Performance Under Load**: Scalable applications maintain performance during peak usage, ensuring a smooth user experience even during surges in demand.
- **Cost-Effectiveness**: Organizations can optimize their resources by scaling up or out as needed, avoiding overprovisioning and unnecessary costs.
- **Flexibility**: A scalable architecture allows organizations to quickly adapt to changing market conditions or user demands.

2. Understanding Security Resilience

Definition:

Security resilience refers to an organization's ability to prepare for, respond to, and recover from security incidents while maintaining operational continuity. A resilient system can withstand attacks and other disruptions, minimizing the impact on business operations.

Components of Security Resilience:

- **Prevention**: Implementing security measures to prevent attacks before they occur. This includes threat detection, access controls, and vulnerability management.
- **Detection**: Real-time monitoring of systems to identify and respond to potential security threats. Effective detection mechanisms are crucial for mitigating the impact of incidents.
- **Response**: Developing incident response plans that outline how to react to security breaches or disruptions. A well-defined response strategy ensures that teams can act quickly to contain incidents and restore services.
- **Recovery**: Ensuring that systems can recover from attacks or outages, including data backups, failover strategies, and business continuity planning.

Importance of Security Resilience:

- **Minimized Downtime**: A resilient application can quickly recover from security incidents, reducing downtime and maintaining service availability.
- **Protection of Sensitive Data**: By being prepared for attacks, organizations can better protect sensitive data and comply with regulations.
- **Enhanced Reputation**: Organizations that demonstrate resilience in the face of security threats build trust with users and stakeholders, enhancing their reputation in the market.

3. Integrating Scalability and Security Resilience in Design

Creating a design that incorporates both scalability and security resilience requires a strategic approach. Below are best practices and considerations for achieving this integration:

Microservices Architecture:

Adopting a microservices architecture enables horizontal scalability by allowing individual services to scale independently. This not only enhances performance but also improves resilience, as a failure in one service does not affect the entire application.

Load Balancing:

Implementing load balancers helps distribute incoming traffic across multiple servers, ensuring that no single server is overwhelmed. This approach enhances both scalability and availability, as traffic can be rerouted to healthy instances in the event of a failure.

Caching Strategies:

Utilize caching mechanisms to reduce the load on backend systems. By storing frequently accessed data in memory, applications can handle higher traffic volumes while maintaining fast response times.

Automated Scaling:

Implement auto-scaling features that automatically adjust resources based on current demand. This ensures that the application can efficiently scale up during peak times and scale down during periods of low demand, optimizing resource utilization.

Security by Design:

Incorporate security considerations into the design phase of the application lifecycle. This includes threat modeling, secure coding practices, and regular security assessments to identify and mitigate vulnerabilities early in development.

Resilient Infrastructure:

Build resilience into the underlying infrastructure by leveraging redundancy, failover strategies, and disaster recovery plans. This can involve using multiple data centers, redundant network paths, and automated backups to ensure operational continuity.

Monitoring and Analytics:

Implement comprehensive monitoring and analytics tools to gain visibility into application performance and security. This enables organizations to detect anomalies, identify potential threats, and make informed decisions about scaling needs.

Incident Response Plans:

Develop and regularly update incident response plans that address various security scenarios. Conduct tabletop exercises to ensure that teams are prepared to act quickly and effectively in the event of a security breach.

Data Protection Measures:

Ensure that sensitive data is protected through encryption, both at rest and in transit. Employ data loss prevention (DLP) solutions to monitor and protect sensitive information from unauthorized access.

Regular Testing and Auditing:

Conduct regular performance and security testing, including load testing, penetration testing, and vulnerability assessments. These practices help identify weaknesses and ensure that the application can handle growth while maintaining security.

Designing applications with scalability and security resilience in mind is essential for navigating the complexities of today's digital landscape. By understanding the principles of scalability and security resilience, organizations can create systems that not only handle growth effectively but also withstand and recover from security incidents. Integrating these concepts into the design phase of application development enables organizations to build robust, adaptable, and secure applications that meet the demands of users and stakeholders alike. As threats continue to evolve, a commitment to scalable and resilient design will be key to maintaining operational integrity and protecting sensitive data in the face of adversity.

9. Continuous Security in DevOps (DevSecOps)

In Continuous Security in DevOps (DevSecOps), we delve into the integration of security practices within the DevOps framework to create a culture of continuous security throughout the software development lifecycle. This chapter discusses the principles of shifting security left, enabling developers to identify and address vulnerabilities early in the development process. We explore strategies for integrating security into continuous integration and continuous deployment (CI/CD) pipelines, emphasizing automated security testing, code analysis, and vulnerability scanning. By fostering collaboration between development, operations, and security teams, organizations can enhance their security posture while maintaining agility and speed, ensuring that security is an ongoing, fundamental aspect of their software development practices.

9.1 Integrating Security into CI/CD Pipelines

In today's fast-paced software development environment, Continuous Integration (CI) and Continuous Deployment (CD) have become essential practices for delivering high-quality software rapidly. However, the increased speed of development also introduces significant security risks, necessitating the integration of security measures throughout the CI/CD pipeline. This section explores the importance of integrating security into CI/CD pipelines, the benefits of doing so, and best practices for achieving a secure development lifecycle.

1. Understanding CI/CD Pipelines

Definition:

A CI/CD pipeline is an automated process that allows developers to integrate code changes frequently (CI) and deploy those changes automatically to production environments (CD). This approach helps teams deliver new features, fixes, and updates quickly and reliably.

Key Components:

- **Continuous Integration (CI):** Involves automatically testing and merging code changes into a shared repository. Automated tests are executed to identify bugs and ensure code quality before integration.

- **Continuous Deployment (CD):** Extends CI by automatically deploying code changes to production after passing CI tests. This ensures that new features and fixes are available to users as quickly as possible.

2. The Importance of Integrating Security

Integrating security into CI/CD pipelines—often referred to as DevSecOps—ensures that security is considered at every stage of the development lifecycle. This approach offers several benefits:

Shift Left Approach: By incorporating security measures early in the development process, organizations can identify and address vulnerabilities before they reach production, reducing remediation costs and improving overall software quality.

Continuous Security Testing: Automated security testing can be integrated into the CI/CD pipeline, allowing for real-time identification of vulnerabilities and compliance issues as code changes are made.

Faster Incident Response: When security is integrated into the development process, teams can respond more rapidly to vulnerabilities and security incidents, minimizing the impact on production systems.

Increased Collaboration: Integrating security fosters collaboration between development, operations, and security teams, creating a shared responsibility for security and encouraging a culture of security awareness.

3. Best Practices for Integrating Security into CI/CD Pipelines

Automated Security Testing:

- **Static Application Security Testing (SAST):** Integrate SAST tools to analyze source code for vulnerabilities and coding standards before code is committed to the repository. This allows for early detection of security issues.
- **Dynamic Application Security Testing (DAST):** Implement DAST tools to test running applications for vulnerabilities during the testing phase of the pipeline. This simulates real-world attacks to identify weaknesses.
- **Software Composition Analysis (SCA):** Use SCA tools to identify vulnerabilities in third-party libraries and dependencies, ensuring that all components of the application are secure.

Security Gate Policies:

- Establish security gates within the CI/CD pipeline that require certain security checks to pass before allowing the code to proceed to the next stage. This can include successful test results from SAST, DAST, and SCA tools.
- Define thresholds for security vulnerabilities that must be met for code changes to be merged or deployed. This helps enforce security standards consistently across the development process.

Infrastructure as Code (IaC) Security:

- Utilize IaC tools to define and manage infrastructure configurations through code. Integrate security checks to validate configurations against security best practices and compliance requirements before deploying infrastructure changes.
- Regularly audit and scan IaC configurations to identify potential security misconfigurations and vulnerabilities.

Automated Compliance Checks:

- Incorporate automated compliance checks into the pipeline to ensure that code and configurations adhere to industry standards and regulatory requirements (e.g., GDPR, HIPAA).
- Use tools that provide compliance reports and alerts to help teams maintain adherence to security policies throughout the development process.

Container Security:

- For organizations using containerization, integrate container security tools into the pipeline to scan container images for vulnerabilities before deployment. This includes checking for outdated libraries and security flaws in the application code.
- Implement runtime security monitoring for containers to detect potential threats and anomalies during deployment.

Secure Secrets Management:

- Avoid hardcoding sensitive information, such as API keys and passwords, into the codebase. Instead, utilize secure secrets management solutions (e.g., HashiCorp Vault, AWS Secrets Manager) to store and manage sensitive data securely.
- Ensure that secrets are only accessible to the components that need them and are rotated regularly to minimize the risk of exposure.

Monitoring and Logging:

- Implement comprehensive monitoring and logging practices to gain visibility into the CI/CD pipeline and production environment. This allows teams to detect and respond to security incidents quickly.
- Set up alerts for unusual activities or security events, enabling rapid investigation and response.

Security Training and Awareness:

- Provide regular training and resources to developers and operations teams on secure coding practices and security tools used within the CI/CD pipeline. This promotes a culture of security awareness and empowers teams to take ownership of security in their work.
- Encourage developers to stay informed about the latest security trends, vulnerabilities, and best practices to foster a proactive security mindset.

Incident Response Planning:

- Develop and document incident response plans that outline how to respond to security incidents detected in the CI/CD pipeline or production environment. This includes defining roles and responsibilities, communication protocols, and escalation procedures.
- Conduct tabletop exercises and simulations to test the effectiveness of the incident response plan and ensure that teams are prepared to act swiftly in the event of a security breach.

Integrating security into CI/CD pipelines is no longer optional; it is a necessity in today's fast-paced development environment. By adopting a DevSecOps approach and implementing best practices, organizations can ensure that security is embedded into every stage of the development lifecycle. This proactive stance not only enhances the security posture of applications but also fosters a culture of collaboration and shared responsibility among development, operations, and security teams. As the landscape of software development continues to evolve, the integration of security into CI/CD pipelines will be crucial for maintaining robust, secure, and resilient applications that can withstand the challenges of modern cyber threats.

9.2 Automated Security Testing and Vulnerability Scanning

In the rapidly evolving landscape of software development, security must be a continuous consideration rather than an afterthought. Automated security testing and vulnerability scanning are essential practices for identifying and addressing potential security issues early in the software development lifecycle (SDLC). This section explores the significance of these practices, the different types of automated security testing and scanning tools, and best practices for their implementation.

1. The Importance of Automated Security Testing and Vulnerability Scanning

Proactive Security Posture:

Automated security testing and vulnerability scanning allow organizations to adopt a proactive security posture. By identifying vulnerabilities early in the development process, teams can mitigate risks before they reach production, thereby reducing the likelihood of security breaches.

Increased Efficiency:

Manual security testing is often time-consuming and prone to human error. Automating security tests and scans improves efficiency, allowing security teams to focus on analyzing results and addressing identified issues rather than conducting repetitive tasks.

Continuous Integration:

Integrating automated security testing and vulnerability scanning into Continuous Integration/Continuous Deployment (CI/CD) pipelines enables continuous monitoring for security issues. This ensures that security is an integral part of the development process, aligning with the principles of DevSecOps.

Regulatory Compliance:

Many industries are subject to regulatory requirements that mandate regular security assessments and vulnerability scans. Automating these processes helps organizations demonstrate compliance and maintain adherence to industry standards.

2. Types of Automated Security Testing

Static Application Security Testing (SAST):

Definition: SAST tools analyze source code or binary code for vulnerabilities without executing the application. This testing occurs early in the development process and identifies issues such as coding flaws, insecure configurations, and potential vulnerabilities.

Benefits:

- Early detection of vulnerabilities in the codebase.
- Comprehensive analysis of all code paths, ensuring thorough testing.
- Integration into IDEs for real-time feedback to developers.

Common Tools: Checkmarx, Fortify, SonarQube, Veracode.

Dynamic Application Security Testing (DAST):

Definition: DAST tools assess the application while it is running. These tools simulate real-world attacks to identify vulnerabilities such as SQL injection, cross-site scripting (XSS), and other runtime issues.

Benefits:

- Detection of vulnerabilities that may not be visible in static analysis, such as those related to server configuration or user input.
- Testing of the application's response to simulated attacks, providing insights into potential exploitability.

Common Tools: OWASP ZAP, Burp Suite, Acunetix.

Interactive Application Security Testing (IAST):

Definition: IAST combines elements of both SAST and DAST by analyzing code in real-time while the application is being tested. This approach allows for more accurate identification of vulnerabilities during the testing phase.

Benefits:

- Comprehensive coverage by combining static and dynamic analysis.
- Immediate feedback during runtime, helping developers address issues as they arise.

Common Tools: Contrast Security, Seeker, Veracode IAST.

Software Composition Analysis (SCA):

Definition: SCA tools identify and analyze open-source components and third-party libraries used in the application. They check for known vulnerabilities in these components and assess licensing compliance.

Benefits:

- Detection of vulnerabilities in third-party libraries that may introduce risks.
- Ensuring compliance with licensing requirements for open-source components.

Common Tools: Snyk, Black Duck, WhiteSource.

3. Vulnerability Scanning

Definition:

Vulnerability scanning involves the automated assessment of systems, networks, and applications to identify known vulnerabilities. This process can help organizations uncover weaknesses before they are exploited by attackers.

Types of Vulnerability Scanning:

Network Vulnerability Scanning:

- **Purpose**: Scans network devices, servers, and firewalls for known vulnerabilities, misconfigurations, and compliance issues.
- **Benefits**: Provides an overview of the security posture of the network and helps identify devices that require remediation.

Common Tools: Nessus, Qualys, OpenVAS.

Web Application Vulnerability Scanning:

- **Purpose**: Specifically targets web applications to identify vulnerabilities such as SQL injection, cross-site scripting, and insecure configurations.

- **Benefits**: Helps organizations secure their web applications before they go live or after updates.

Common Tools: Burp Suite, Acunetix, Netsparker.

Cloud Vulnerability Scanning:

- **Purpose**: Assesses cloud infrastructure and services for misconfigurations and vulnerabilities specific to cloud environments.
- **Benefits**: Ensures that cloud deployments are secure and compliant with security best practices.

Common Tools: Prisma Cloud, AWS Inspector, Azure Security Center.

4. Best Practices for Implementing Automated Security Testing and Vulnerability Scanning

Integrate into CI/CD Pipelines:

- Incorporate automated security testing and vulnerability scanning tools into the CI/CD pipeline to ensure continuous monitoring for security issues.
- Establish security gates that require successful test results before code can move to the next stage of the pipeline.

Prioritize Vulnerabilities:

- Use risk-based prioritization to focus on addressing the most critical vulnerabilities first. This ensures that the most severe issues are resolved before less critical ones.
- Utilize Common Vulnerability Scoring System (CVSS) scores to assess the severity of vulnerabilities.

Regularly Update Tools:

Keep security testing and scanning tools up to date to ensure that they can detect the latest vulnerabilities. Regular updates also help maintain compliance with security standards.

Combine Different Testing Approaches:

Use a combination of SAST, DAST, IAST, and SCA tools to achieve comprehensive coverage of the application. Each approach has its strengths and weaknesses, and using multiple tools can provide a more thorough assessment.

Continuous Monitoring:

Implement continuous monitoring of production environments to identify vulnerabilities that may arise post-deployment. This is crucial for maintaining ongoing security and compliance.

Educate Development Teams:

Provide training and resources to development teams on secure coding practices and the importance of security testing. This fosters a culture of security awareness and encourages developers to prioritize security in their work.

Maintain an Incident Response Plan:

Establish an incident response plan to address vulnerabilities that are discovered during testing or scanning. This plan should outline roles, responsibilities, and procedures for addressing and remediating security incidents.

Document and Track Findings:

Maintain a detailed record of vulnerabilities identified during testing and scanning, along with remediation efforts. This documentation can help track progress and ensure that issues are addressed in a timely manner.

Automated security testing and vulnerability scanning are critical components of a robust security strategy in modern software development. By integrating these practices into the CI/CD pipeline, organizations can proactively identify and address vulnerabilities throughout the development lifecycle. This not only enhances the security posture of applications but also fosters a culture of security awareness among development teams. As cyber threats continue to evolve, adopting automated security testing and vulnerability scanning practices will be essential for organizations seeking to deliver secure, high-quality software in an increasingly competitive landscape.

9.3 Shift-Left Security: Bringing Security Early into DevOps

As organizations increasingly adopt DevOps methodologies to enhance collaboration, streamline processes, and accelerate delivery, the integration of security within this framework has become paramount. The concept of "Shift-Left Security" emphasizes the importance of incorporating security measures early in the software development lifecycle (SDLC), shifting the focus from traditional post-development security assessments to proactive, continuous security practices. This section explores the principles of Shift-Left Security, its benefits, and best practices for implementation.

1. Understanding Shift-Left Security

Definition:

Shift-Left Security refers to the practice of integrating security processes and testing early in the software development lifecycle. By addressing security concerns at the earliest stages of development, teams can identify vulnerabilities and potential threats before they escalate into significant issues in production.

Historical Context:

Traditionally, security assessments occurred towards the end of the development cycle, often resulting in delays, increased costs, and heightened risks. With the Shift-Left approach, security becomes a shared responsibility among development, operations, and security teams, fostering a culture of security awareness and collaboration.

2. Benefits of Shift-Left Security

Early Detection of Vulnerabilities:

By identifying vulnerabilities early in the development process, teams can remediate issues before they become more complex and costly to fix. This approach minimizes the likelihood of security breaches and reduces overall risk.

Cost-Effective Remediation:

Fixing vulnerabilities early is significantly less expensive than addressing them after deployment. Studies have shown that the cost of addressing security flaws increases exponentially as development progresses, making early detection essential for cost control.

Enhanced Collaboration:

Shift-Left Security promotes collaboration between development, operations, and security teams. This alignment encourages knowledge sharing and a unified approach to security, leading to more secure software development practices.

Continuous Security Culture:

By integrating security into daily development practices, organizations foster a culture of continuous security awareness. Developers become more mindful of security best practices, reducing the likelihood of introducing vulnerabilities into the codebase.

Faster Time to Market:

With security integrated early in the process, development teams can avoid the bottlenecks often caused by late-stage security testing. This streamlining allows for faster delivery of secure software to customers.

3. Implementing Shift-Left Security

Incorporate Security into Agile Development:

- Integrate security practices into Agile development methodologies by including security requirements in user stories and defining acceptance criteria that encompass security considerations.
- Conduct regular security reviews during sprint planning and retrospectives to ensure security is a priority.

Automated Security Testing:

- Implement automated security testing tools (e.g., SAST, DAST, SCA) within CI/CD pipelines to identify vulnerabilities continuously as code changes are made.
- Provide developers with real-time feedback on security issues, enabling them to address concerns immediately.

Security Training and Awareness:

- Provide ongoing security training for developers to enhance their understanding of secure coding practices and threat modeling. This training empowers developers to make informed decisions regarding security as they write code.

- Foster a culture of security awareness by encouraging developers to share security knowledge and best practices within the team.

Threat Modeling:

- Incorporate threat modeling sessions early in the design phase of development. By identifying potential threats and vulnerabilities in the architectural design, teams can make informed decisions to mitigate risks.
- Utilize threat modeling frameworks (e.g., STRIDE, PASTA) to guide the process and ensure comprehensive coverage of potential security risks.

Use of Secure Code Libraries:

- Encourage the use of secure coding libraries and frameworks that adhere to best practices. This can help developers avoid common pitfalls and vulnerabilities associated with custom code.
- Regularly update libraries and dependencies to patch known vulnerabilities and reduce exposure to risks.

Continuous Monitoring and Feedback:

- Implement continuous monitoring of applications in production to detect vulnerabilities and security incidents in real time. This can include logging, anomaly detection, and security information and event management (SIEM) systems.
- Establish feedback loops to inform development teams of security findings and trends, enabling them to make informed decisions for future development cycles.

Collaborative Security Reviews:

- Conduct regular collaborative security reviews involving developers, security teams, and operations personnel. These reviews help identify security gaps and align security practices with development workflows.
- Use these sessions to share lessons learned from previous security incidents and encourage open discussions about security challenges and solutions.

Security Gates in CI/CD Pipelines:

- Establish security gates within CI/CD pipelines that require successful completion of security tests before code can be merged or deployed. This reinforces the importance of security at every stage of development.

- Define thresholds for vulnerabilities that must be met for code to progress through the pipeline, ensuring consistent adherence to security standards.

4. Challenges and Considerations

Cultural Resistance:

Shifting to a Shift-Left Security approach may face resistance from development teams accustomed to traditional workflows. To overcome this, organizations should prioritize change management, emphasizing the benefits of early security integration.

Tool Integration:

Integrating security tools into existing CI/CD pipelines can be complex. Organizations should carefully evaluate and select tools that align with their development environment and workflows.

Balancing Speed and Security:

Striking a balance between rapid development and thorough security practices can be challenging. Teams must prioritize automation and efficiency while ensuring that security remains a top priority.

Resource Allocation:

Ensuring adequate resources for security training, tool implementation, and continuous monitoring is essential. Organizations should allocate budget and personnel to support ongoing security initiatives.

Shift-Left Security represents a paradigm shift in how organizations approach software security. By integrating security practices early in the development lifecycle, teams can proactively identify and address vulnerabilities, fostering a culture of collaboration and continuous improvement. This approach not only enhances the security posture of applications but also accelerates the delivery of secure software, ultimately resulting in greater trust from customers and stakeholders. As cyber threats continue to evolve, the adoption of Shift-Left Security will be crucial for organizations seeking to navigate the complexities of modern software development securely.

10. Penetration Testing and Code Reviews

In Penetration Testing and Code Reviews, we focus on essential practices that help identify and remediate vulnerabilities in software applications. This chapter provides an overview of penetration testing, including its methodologies and types, enabling developers to understand how to simulate real-world attacks to assess their software's security posture. We also cover the importance of regular code reviews as a means of discovering security flaws early in the development process, highlighting techniques for effective peer reviews and the use of static and dynamic analysis tools. By incorporating both penetration testing and thorough code reviews into their development practices, teams can proactively uncover security weaknesses, ensuring that their applications are fortified against potential threats and vulnerabilities before deployment.

10.1 Fundamentals of Penetration Testing for Developers

In today's digital landscape, software applications are increasingly becoming targets for cyber threats. As developers strive to create robust, secure software, understanding the fundamentals of penetration testing is essential. Penetration testing, or pen testing, is a critical component of a comprehensive security strategy. It involves simulating real-world attacks to identify vulnerabilities within applications, networks, and systems. This section will explore the basics of penetration testing, its importance for developers, the various methodologies involved, and best practices for integrating it into the development lifecycle.

1. Understanding Penetration Testing

Definition:

Penetration testing is a simulated cyberattack carried out by security professionals (penetration testers) to assess the security of an application, system, or network. The primary goal is to identify vulnerabilities that an attacker could exploit, providing organizations with insights into their security posture.

Types of Penetration Testing:

Black Box Testing:

- The tester has no prior knowledge of the system architecture or source code. This approach mimics an external attacker who has no insider information.
- Black box testing is useful for identifying vulnerabilities that an outsider might exploit.

White Box Testing:

- The tester has full access to the system's architecture, source code, and documentation. This approach allows for a more thorough assessment of potential vulnerabilities.
- White box testing helps identify issues that may not be evident from an external perspective.

Gray Box Testing:

- The tester has limited knowledge of the system, simulating a scenario where an attacker has some insider information (e.g., through social engineering).
- Gray box testing offers a balanced perspective by focusing on both external and internal vulnerabilities.

2. The Importance of Penetration Testing for Developers

Identifying Vulnerabilities:

Penetration testing enables developers to discover security flaws that could be exploited by malicious actors. Early identification allows for timely remediation, reducing the risk of breaches.

Understanding Attack Vectors:

By simulating real-world attacks, developers gain insights into potential attack vectors that could be used against their applications. This understanding helps in designing more secure software.

Improving Security Awareness:

Engaging in penetration testing fosters a culture of security awareness within development teams. Developers learn to think like attackers, leading to better coding practices and proactive security measures.

Validating Security Controls:

Penetration testing validates the effectiveness of security controls implemented in the application. It helps organizations understand whether their security measures are adequate to withstand attacks.

Regulatory Compliance:

Many industries require regular penetration testing as part of compliance with regulations and standards (e.g., PCI DSS, HIPAA). Conducting these tests helps organizations demonstrate adherence to security best practices.

3. The Penetration Testing Process

Planning and Scope Definition:

- **Define Objectives**: Determine the goals of the penetration test, such as identifying vulnerabilities, testing specific features, or assessing compliance.
- **Establish Scope**: Clearly define the boundaries of the test, including which systems, applications, and networks will be included. Ensure all stakeholders are informed and agree on the scope.

Information Gathering:

- **Passive Reconnaissance**: Collect information about the target system through publicly available sources, such as domain registrations, social media, and public forums.
- **Active Reconnaissance**: Use tools to gather detailed information about the target, such as network scans, port scans, and service enumeration.

Threat Modeling:

Analyze the gathered information to identify potential threats and attack vectors. Create a threat model that outlines the most likely attack scenarios and their impact.

Exploitation:

- Attempt to exploit identified vulnerabilities to determine their impact. This phase involves using various techniques and tools to gain unauthorized access, escalate privileges, or exfiltrate data.

- Ensure that exploitation is conducted ethically and that all actions are documented for later analysis.

Post-Exploitation:

- Assess the extent of access gained during exploitation. Identify sensitive data, user accounts, and critical systems that could be compromised.
- Document findings and determine the potential impact of a successful attack.

Reporting:

- Compile a comprehensive report detailing the findings, including identified vulnerabilities, methods used, and recommendations for remediation. The report should be clear and actionable, aimed at both technical and non-technical stakeholders.
- Include an executive summary highlighting critical risks and the overall security posture.

Remediation and Retesting:

- Collaborate with development teams to address identified vulnerabilities. Implement fixes, patches, and improvements based on the findings.
- Conduct retesting to ensure that vulnerabilities have been adequately addressed and that security controls are functioning as intended.

4. Best Practices for Developers in Penetration Testing

Involve Security from the Start:

Integrate security practices and penetration testing into the software development lifecycle (SDLC) from the outset. This proactive approach enhances the security posture of applications.

Collaborate with Security Teams:

Foster collaboration between development and security teams. Involve security professionals in the design and development phases to identify potential vulnerabilities early.

Utilize Automated Tools:

Leverage automated penetration testing tools to streamline the testing process and enhance efficiency. Tools like Burp Suite, Metasploit, and OWASP ZAP can assist in identifying vulnerabilities and automating certain aspects of the testing.

Educate Developers:

Provide ongoing training for developers on secure coding practices and the principles of penetration testing. Awareness of common vulnerabilities (e.g., OWASP Top Ten) equips developers to write more secure code.

Establish a Security Testing Environment:

Set up a dedicated testing environment for penetration testing that mirrors production as closely as possible. This allows for safe testing without impacting live systems.

Document Findings and Improvements:

Maintain detailed records of penetration tests, findings, and remediation efforts. This documentation serves as a valuable resource for future testing and helps track the progress of security improvements.

Regularly Conduct Penetration Tests:

Make penetration testing a regular part of the security strategy. Conduct tests after major code releases, architectural changes, or significant updates to ensure ongoing security.

Embrace a Continuous Learning Approach:

Stay informed about emerging threats, vulnerabilities, and testing methodologies. Encourage a culture of continuous learning and improvement within the development team.

Penetration testing is a vital practice for developers aiming to build secure software in an increasingly hostile cyber environment. By understanding the fundamentals of penetration testing, developers can proactively identify and remediate vulnerabilities, ultimately enhancing the security of their applications. Integrating penetration testing into the software development lifecycle fosters a culture of security awareness, enabling teams to deliver robust, secure solutions that meet the demands of modern users. As cyber threats continue to evolve, the commitment to penetration testing and continuous security practices will be essential for organizations seeking to protect their assets and maintain customer trust.

10.2 Using Static and Dynamic Code Analysis Tools

In the realm of secure software development, ensuring code quality and security is paramount. One of the most effective ways to achieve this is through the use of code analysis tools. These tools can be broadly categorized into two types: Static Code Analysis (SCA) and Dynamic Code Analysis (DCA). Each type serves a unique purpose in the software development lifecycle, enabling developers to identify vulnerabilities and ensure compliance with security standards. This section will delve into the principles, benefits, and best practices associated with both static and dynamic code analysis tools.

1. Understanding Static Code Analysis (SCA)

Definition:

Static code analysis involves examining the source code of an application without executing it. This type of analysis is typically performed early in the software development lifecycle, allowing developers to identify potential vulnerabilities, coding errors, and non-compliance with coding standards before the code is compiled or executed.

How Static Code Analysis Works:

SCA tools parse the source code and create an abstract representation of the code structure. They then apply a set of predefined rules or heuristics to identify potential issues. These rules can range from simple syntax checks to complex security vulnerabilities.

Common Static Code Analysis Tools:

- **SonarQube**: An open-source platform for continuous inspection of code quality that performs automatic reviews with static analysis.
- **Checkmarx**: A comprehensive SCA tool that identifies security vulnerabilities and compliance issues in the code.
- **FindBugs/SpotBugs**: A static analysis tool that detects potential bugs in Java programs.
- **ESLint**: A popular tool for identifying and fixing problems in JavaScript code by enforcing coding standards and best practices.

2. Benefits of Static Code Analysis

Early Detection of Vulnerabilities:

By identifying vulnerabilities during the coding phase, developers can address issues before they escalate, reducing the risk of security breaches in production.

Improved Code Quality:

SCA tools help enforce coding standards and best practices, leading to cleaner, more maintainable code. This not only enhances security but also improves overall software quality.

Cost-Effective Remediation:

Fixing issues identified through static analysis is generally less costly than addressing them after deployment. Early detection leads to significant savings in time and resources.

Automation:

Static code analysis can be easily integrated into the Continuous Integration/Continuous Deployment (CI/CD) pipeline, providing automated feedback to developers as they write code.

Comprehensive Coverage:

SCA tools can analyze large codebases quickly, ensuring that all parts of the code are evaluated for vulnerabilities, including those that may be overlooked during manual code reviews.

3. Limitations of Static Code Analysis

False Positives:

SCA tools may generate false positives—issues that are flagged as vulnerabilities but do not pose a real threat. This can lead to alert fatigue among developers if not managed properly.

Lack of Context:

Static analysis does not consider the runtime behavior of the application, which can lead to a lack of context in certain scenarios. Some vulnerabilities may only be evident during execution.

Limited Scope:

While SCA is effective at identifying coding issues and vulnerabilities, it may not capture all types of security risks, especially those related to application configuration or runtime behavior.

4. Understanding Dynamic Code Analysis (DCA)

Definition:

Dynamic code analysis, on the other hand, involves evaluating an application during its execution. This approach allows developers to identify vulnerabilities and security issues that manifest during runtime, providing a different perspective compared to static analysis.

How Dynamic Code Analysis Works:

DCA tools monitor the application's behavior in a runtime environment. They can identify issues such as memory leaks, input validation errors, and security vulnerabilities like SQL injection and cross-site scripting (XSS). Dynamic analysis can be performed in a controlled environment (e.g., a staging server) or against a production-like setup.

Common Dynamic Code Analysis Tools:

- **OWASP ZAP (Zed Attack Proxy):** An open-source dynamic application security testing (DAST) tool used to find vulnerabilities in web applications.
- **Burp Suite**: A comprehensive web vulnerability scanner that provides dynamic testing capabilities.
- **AppScan**: A commercial tool that identifies vulnerabilities in web applications by simulating real-world attacks.
- **Netsparker**: A dynamic web application security scanner that automatically identifies vulnerabilities in web applications.

5. Benefits of Dynamic Code Analysis

Real-World Testing:

DCA simulates real-world attacks on the application, allowing for the identification of vulnerabilities that may not be evident in static analysis.

Comprehensive Vulnerability Detection:

Dynamic analysis can identify issues related to application configuration, server-side logic, and user interactions that static analysis might miss.

Behavioral Insights:

DCA provides insights into how the application behaves under various conditions, enabling developers to identify performance bottlenecks and security weaknesses in real-time.

Security Validation:

Running dynamic tests helps validate the effectiveness of security controls implemented in the application, ensuring that they work as intended in a live environment.

6. Limitations of Dynamic Code Analysis

Environment Dependency:

DCA results can vary significantly based on the environment in which the tests are conducted. Issues identified in a testing environment may not always be present in production.

Increased Complexity:

Setting up and configuring dynamic analysis tools can be more complex than static analysis, often requiring significant resources and expertise.

Potential Performance Impact:

Running dynamic tests can impact the performance of the application, especially if conducted in a production environment. This necessitates careful planning and scheduling.

7. Integrating Static and Dynamic Code Analysis into Development Practices

To maximize the benefits of both static and dynamic code analysis tools, developers should consider the following best practices:

Choose the Right Tools:

Evaluate and select SCA and DCA tools that best fit the organization's technology stack, budget, and specific security requirements.

Integrate into CI/CD Pipelines:

Automate the use of static analysis tools within CI/CD pipelines to ensure code is continuously evaluated for security vulnerabilities during development.

Conduct Regular Dynamic Testing:

Schedule regular dynamic analysis tests as part of the software development lifecycle, particularly before major releases or after significant code changes.

Train Development Teams:

Provide training on how to effectively use static and dynamic analysis tools. This training should also include how to interpret results and implement fixes.

Establish Clear Reporting and Remediation Processes:

Create processes for handling the findings from both static and dynamic analysis, including documentation, remediation tracking, and retesting.

Foster a Security Culture:

Encourage a culture of security within development teams by promoting awareness of security vulnerabilities and the importance of secure coding practices.

Use Both Methods in Combination:

Recognize that static and dynamic analysis complement each other. Use both methods to achieve comprehensive security coverage, as each tool type addresses different aspects of application security.

Utilizing static and dynamic code analysis tools is essential for developers committed to building secure software. By incorporating these tools into the software development lifecycle, organizations can proactively identify and mitigate vulnerabilities, enhance code quality, and ensure compliance with security standards. While both static and dynamic analysis have their strengths and limitations, their combined use provides a comprehensive approach to application security, ultimately leading to more resilient software in an increasingly complex threat landscape. Embracing these practices not only strengthens the security posture of applications but also cultivates a culture of security awareness among developers, ensuring that security remains a priority throughout the development process.

10.3 Conducting Effective Security Code Reviews

In the quest for building secure software, security code reviews serve as a critical line of defense. They are an essential practice that allows developers to examine the source code for vulnerabilities and security weaknesses before the software is deployed. A well-executed security code review can help identify and mitigate potential security risks, ensuring that applications are robust against malicious attacks. This section outlines the principles, methodologies, and best practices for conducting effective security code reviews.

1. Understanding the Purpose of Security Code Reviews

Definition:

A security code review is a systematic examination of the source code by one or more developers (or security experts) with the intent of identifying security vulnerabilities, coding errors, and compliance issues. The primary goal is to improve the security posture of the application by uncovering issues that static and dynamic analysis tools may not detect.

Benefits of Security Code Reviews:

- **Early Detection of Vulnerabilities**: Identifying vulnerabilities during the code review phase allows for timely remediation, reducing the risk of security breaches in production.
- **Knowledge Sharing**: Code reviews foster collaboration among team members, encouraging knowledge sharing about secure coding practices and common vulnerabilities.

- **Improved Code Quality**: Security reviews contribute to overall code quality by enforcing coding standards and best practices, leading to more maintainable and secure code.
- **Enhanced Security Awareness**: Engaging in regular code reviews promotes a culture of security awareness within the development team, helping developers think critically about security issues.

2. Key Principles for Effective Security Code Reviews

Incorporate Security from the Start:

Begin security code reviews early in the development process, ideally during the design and implementation phases. This proactive approach helps identify security issues before they become ingrained in the codebase.

Define Clear Objectives:

Establish clear goals for the code review process. This could include identifying specific vulnerabilities, ensuring compliance with security standards, or improving overall code quality.

Utilize a Structured Approach:

Adopt a systematic methodology for conducting code reviews, which includes well-defined processes, checklists, and tools. This ensures consistency and thoroughness in the review process.

Focus on High-Risk Areas:

Pay special attention to high-risk areas of the code, such as authentication, authorization, data handling, and input validation. These areas are often targeted by attackers and require extra scrutiny.

3. Methodologies for Conducting Security Code Reviews

Manual Code Reviews:

Manual reviews involve developers examining the code line by line to identify vulnerabilities. This method is effective for uncovering complex issues that automated tools may miss.

Best Practices for Manual Reviews:

- Establish a team of reviewers with diverse skill sets to provide multiple perspectives.
- Use a checklist of common vulnerabilities (e.g., OWASP Top Ten) to guide the review process.
- Encourage open communication and discussion among team members to facilitate knowledge sharing.

Automated Code Reviews:

Automated tools can help streamline the code review process by identifying vulnerabilities and coding errors in real time. Tools such as SonarQube, Fortify, and Checkmarx can be integrated into the development workflow.

Best Practices for Automated Reviews:

- Select the right tools that fit the technology stack and specific needs of the project.
- Configure the tools to align with coding standards and best practices relevant to the organization.
- Review the findings of automated tools with a critical eye, as they may produce false positives or overlook contextual issues.

Peer Reviews:

In peer reviews, team members review each other's code. This fosters collaboration and encourages developers to learn from one another's expertise.

Best Practices for Peer Reviews:

- Pair developers with different levels of experience to facilitate mentorship and knowledge sharing.
- Set a positive tone for the review process, emphasizing constructive feedback over criticism.
- Ensure that reviews are conducted regularly and in a timely manner to avoid bottlenecks in the development process.

4. Best Practices for Conducting Security Code Reviews

Create a Security Review Checklist:

Develop a checklist of common security issues and best practices that reviewers can reference during the code review process. This checklist should cover areas such as:

- Input validation and output encoding
- Authentication and authorization mechanisms
- Secure data storage and transmission
- Error handling and logging practices

Use Version Control Systems:

Utilize version control systems (e.g., Git) to facilitate collaboration and maintain a history of code changes. This enables reviewers to examine the context of code changes and understand the rationale behind them.

Encourage Continuous Learning:

Foster a culture of continuous learning by providing training on secure coding practices and common vulnerabilities. Encourage team members to stay updated on emerging security threats and trends.

Document Findings and Remediation Efforts:

Maintain detailed records of security findings from code reviews, including the vulnerabilities identified, proposed fixes, and the status of remediation efforts. This documentation serves as a valuable resource for future reviews and audits.

Establish a Feedback Loop:

Create a feedback loop to communicate the results of code reviews back to developers. This can include both positive feedback for secure coding practices and constructive criticism for areas needing improvement.

Integrate Reviews into CI/CD Pipelines:

Incorporate security code reviews into the CI/CD pipeline to ensure that code is continuously evaluated for security vulnerabilities. This allows for immediate feedback and quicker remediation.

Conduct Regular Training Sessions:

Schedule regular training sessions on secure coding practices and effective code review techniques. This ensures that all team members are equipped with the knowledge and skills needed to conduct thorough reviews.

Prioritize Remediation Efforts:

Establish a process for prioritizing the remediation of identified vulnerabilities based on their severity and potential impact on the application. Focus on addressing critical issues first.

Conducting effective security code reviews is a vital component of a comprehensive security strategy. By systematically examining source code for vulnerabilities, organizations can identify and mitigate potential security risks early in the development process. By employing a combination of manual and automated reviews, fostering collaboration among team members, and adhering to best practices, developers can enhance the security posture of their applications. Emphasizing the importance of security code reviews not only improves software quality but also cultivates a culture of security awareness within development teams. In an increasingly complex threat landscape, a commitment to rigorous security code reviews is essential for building resilient software that can withstand malicious attacks.

11. Incident Response and Patch Management

In Incident Response and Patch Management, we explore the critical processes required to effectively address security incidents and maintain the integrity of software systems. This chapter outlines the components of an incident response plan, detailing steps for preparation, detection, containment, eradication, and recovery, ensuring that teams are well-equipped to respond swiftly to security breaches. We also emphasize the importance of establishing clear communication channels and roles within the incident response team. Additionally, we delve into patch management strategies, discussing best practices for timely application of security updates, prioritizing vulnerabilities based on risk, and maintaining an organized inventory of software assets. By implementing robust incident response and patch management protocols, organizations can minimize damage, reduce recovery time, and enhance their overall security posture.

11.1 Creating an Incident Response Plan for Software Teams

In today's digital landscape, the potential for security incidents is ever-present, making it crucial for software development teams to have a robust Incident Response Plan (IRP). An effective IRP helps organizations prepare for, respond to, and recover from security breaches or other critical incidents. This section outlines the steps for creating an effective incident response plan tailored for software teams, ensuring they are well-equipped to handle security events and minimize their impact on business operations.

1. Understanding Incident Response

Definition:

An Incident Response Plan is a documented strategy that outlines how an organization will detect, respond to, manage, and recover from a security incident. The plan serves as a guide for software teams in identifying vulnerabilities, containing threats, and restoring services promptly while minimizing damage.

Importance of an IRP:

- **Preparedness**: An effective IRP ensures that teams are prepared to respond quickly and efficiently to security incidents.

- **Minimized Damage**: A well-structured response can significantly reduce the impact of an incident, including financial loss, reputational damage, and operational disruption.
- **Compliance**: Many industries require organizations to have an IRP in place to meet regulatory compliance standards.
- **Continuous Improvement**: Reviewing and updating the IRP after an incident provides valuable insights for improving processes and preventing future occurrences.

2. Key Components of an Incident Response Plan

Preparation:

- **Establish an Incident Response Team (IRT):** Form a dedicated team responsible for managing incidents. This team should include representatives from various departments, such as development, operations, security, and management.
- **Define Roles and Responsibilities**: Clearly outline the roles and responsibilities of each team member in the IRT. This ensures accountability and efficient communication during an incident.
- **Conduct Training and Awareness Programs**: Regularly train team members on their roles in the incident response process. Conduct awareness programs to educate all employees about security policies and incident reporting procedures.

Identification:

- **Establish Detection Mechanisms**: Implement monitoring tools and processes to detect potential security incidents. This may include intrusion detection systems, log analysis tools, and security information and event management (SIEM) systems.
- **Define Incident Categories**: Create a classification system for incidents based on their severity and impact. This helps prioritize response efforts and allocate resources effectively.

Containment:

- **Immediate Response Protocols**: Outline specific steps for containing the incident to prevent further damage. This may involve isolating affected systems, disabling compromised accounts, or blocking malicious network traffic.

- **Short-Term and Long-Term Containment**: Establish strategies for both immediate containment actions and longer-term measures to prevent recurrence.

Eradication:

- **Identify the Root Cause**: Conduct a thorough investigation to determine the cause of the incident. This involves analyzing logs, conducting interviews, and reviewing system configurations.
- **Remove Threats**: Ensure that all traces of the threat are eliminated from the environment, which may involve applying patches, changing credentials, or deleting malicious files.

Recovery:

- **Restore Systems and Services**: Develop a plan for restoring affected systems and services to normal operation. This may involve restoring backups, reinstalling software, or applying patches.
- **Monitor for Signs of Recurrence**: Implement additional monitoring to detect any signs of the incident reoccurring after recovery efforts.

Lessons Learned:

- **Conduct Post-Incident Analysis**: After resolving the incident, hold a debriefing session with the IRT to discuss what occurred, what was done well, and areas for improvement. This analysis should be documented for future reference.
- **Update the Incident Response Plan**: Use insights gained from the incident to update the IRP and refine response procedures. This ensures continuous improvement and adaptation to evolving threats.

3. Developing the Incident Response Plan

Document the Plan:

Create a comprehensive document outlining the IRP, including the roles, processes, and procedures defined above. The plan should be easily accessible to all team members and regularly updated to reflect changes in technology and organizational structure.

Establish Communication Protocols:

Define how information will be communicated during an incident. This includes internal communication among team members and external communication with stakeholders, clients, and the media. Clear communication is essential for managing the response and maintaining trust.

Testing the Plan:

Regularly test the IRP through simulations and tabletop exercises. These drills help familiarize team members with their roles and allow for identification of gaps in the plan. Testing should occur at least annually or after significant changes to systems or personnel.

Compliance and Legal Considerations:

Ensure that the IRP complies with relevant regulations and legal requirements. This may involve consulting with legal counsel to understand obligations regarding data breaches and reporting requirements.

Integrating with Other Plans:

The IRP should align with other organizational plans, such as disaster recovery and business continuity plans. This integration ensures a cohesive approach to managing incidents and restoring operations.

4. Tools and Resources

Incident Response Platforms:

Invest in tools that assist in managing the incident response process, such as:

- **Incident Management Software**: Tools like PagerDuty or ServiceNow help streamline communication and incident tracking.
- **Forensic Tools**: Software such as EnCase or FTK aids in investigating security incidents and gathering evidence.

Monitoring and Detection Tools:

Implement security monitoring solutions to detect potential incidents, such as:

- **SIEM Solutions**: Tools like Splunk or IBM QRadar provide real-time monitoring and analysis of security events.
- **Intrusion Detection Systems (IDS):** Solutions like Snort or Suricata help identify malicious activities and potential breaches.

Collaboration Tools:

Utilize collaboration platforms to facilitate communication during incidents, such as:

Slack or Microsoft Teams: These tools enable real-time communication and information sharing among incident response team members.

Creating an effective Incident Response Plan is a crucial step for software teams to ensure they are prepared to handle security incidents effectively. By establishing clear processes for preparation, identification, containment, eradication, recovery, and lessons learned, teams can minimize the impact of incidents and enhance their overall security posture. Continuous training, regular testing, and integration with other organizational plans will strengthen the IRP, ensuring that software teams can respond swiftly and effectively to the ever-evolving threat landscape. By investing in an incident response strategy, organizations can not only protect their assets but also instill confidence in their stakeholders, demonstrating a commitment to security and resilience in the face of adversity.

11.2 Detecting and Responding to Security Breaches

In an era where cyber threats are increasing in frequency and sophistication, the ability to detect and respond to security breaches effectively is crucial for organizations. A security breach can have devastating consequences, including financial losses, reputational damage, and legal liabilities. This section outlines strategies and best practices for detecting security breaches, as well as effective response methodologies to minimize their impact and ensure rapid recovery.

1. Understanding Security Breaches

Definition:

A security breach is an incident that results in unauthorized access to, or disclosure of, sensitive data, systems, or networks. This can include data theft, system corruption, denial of service, or other malicious activities aimed at exploiting vulnerabilities.

Types of Security Breaches:

- **Data Breaches**: Unauthorized access to sensitive information, such as personal data or intellectual property.
- **Network Breaches**: Unauthorized access to an organization's network infrastructure, potentially leading to data theft or service disruption.
- **Application Breaches**: Exploitation of vulnerabilities in software applications to gain unauthorized access or perform malicious actions.

2. Detecting Security Breaches

Effective detection of security breaches is the first step in a robust incident response plan. The following strategies can help organizations identify potential breaches:

Implement Security Monitoring Tools:

- **Intrusion Detection Systems (IDS):** Deploy IDS solutions to monitor network traffic for signs of suspicious activity. These systems can alert security teams to potential breaches in real time.
- **Security Information and Event Management (SIEM):** Utilize SIEM solutions to aggregate and analyze security data from various sources. SIEM tools can identify patterns of suspicious behavior and provide alerts for potential breaches.

Establish Baselines for Normal Activity:

Monitor network and system activity to establish baseline behavior. This includes typical user activity patterns, network traffic volumes, and application usage. Deviations from these baselines can indicate potential security breaches.

Conduct Regular Vulnerability Assessments:

Perform regular scans and assessments to identify vulnerabilities in systems and applications. This proactive approach helps organizations address weaknesses before they can be exploited.

Utilize Threat Intelligence:

Integrate threat intelligence feeds to stay informed about emerging threats and vulnerabilities. This information can help organizations adapt their security measures and respond to potential breaches more effectively.

User Behavior Analytics (UBA):

Implement UBA solutions that analyze user activity to detect anomalies, such as unusual login attempts or data access patterns. These tools can help identify compromised accounts or insider threats.

Set Up Alerting Mechanisms:

Configure alerting systems to notify the incident response team of potential security breaches. This may include alerts for unauthorized access attempts, data exfiltration, or changes to critical system configurations.

3. Responding to Security Breaches

Once a security breach has been detected, a swift and organized response is essential. The following steps outline an effective response strategy:

Containment:

- **Immediate Action**: As soon as a breach is detected, the priority should be to contain the incident to prevent further damage. This may involve isolating affected systems, disabling compromised accounts, or blocking malicious network traffic.
- **Short-Term Containment**: Implement temporary measures to limit the breach's impact, such as shutting down affected systems or changing access credentials.
- **Long-Term Containment**: Develop strategies to ensure that the threat is fully eradicated before restoring systems to normal operation.

Assessment and Investigation:

- **Determine the Scope of the Breach**: Assess which systems, data, and users are affected. This may involve examining logs, interviewing personnel, and conducting forensic analysis.
- **Identify the Attack Vector**: Investigate how the breach occurred. Understanding the method of attack is critical for preventing future incidents and informing remediation efforts.

Eradication:

- **Remove the Threat**: Take steps to eliminate the root cause of the breach, whether that involves patching vulnerabilities, removing malware, or reconfiguring systems to enhance security.
- **Secure Systems**: Apply necessary security updates, change passwords, and strengthen access controls to prevent similar incidents.

Recovery:

- **Restore Systems and Data**: Begin the process of restoring affected systems and data from backups, ensuring that all threats have been mitigated. This step must be done cautiously to avoid reintroducing vulnerabilities.
- **Monitor for Recurrence**: Implement enhanced monitoring to detect any signs of the breach reoccurring. This ongoing vigilance is essential during the recovery phase.

Communication:

- **Internal Communication**: Notify relevant stakeholders within the organization about the breach, the response actions being taken, and any changes to policies or procedures.
- **External Communication**: Depending on the severity and impact of the breach, external communication may be necessary. This includes notifying affected customers, regulatory bodies, and the media if required by law or company policy.

Post-Incident Analysis:

- **Conduct a Review**: After the incident is resolved, conduct a thorough review of the breach and the response process. This should involve gathering feedback from the incident response team and documenting lessons learned.
- **Update Incident Response Plan**: Use the insights gained from the analysis to update the Incident Response Plan and improve detection and response strategies for future incidents.

4. Tools and Resources for Detection and Response

Security Monitoring Solutions:

- **SIEM Tools**: Solutions like Splunk, LogRhythm, or IBM QRadar help aggregate security data and provide real-time insights into potential breaches.
- **IDS/IPS Systems**: Tools like Snort or Suricata provide intrusion detection and prevention capabilities to monitor network traffic for suspicious activity.

Forensics and Investigation Tools:

Digital Forensics Software: Tools such as EnCase, FTK, or Volatility are essential for conducting forensic investigations to understand the nature of the breach and gather evidence.

Incident Management Software:

Ticketing Systems: Use software like Jira or ServiceNow to manage incident response efforts, track tasks, and document findings throughout the incident lifecycle.

Threat Intelligence Platforms:

Threat Feeds and Services: Integrate services like Recorded Future or ThreatConnect to stay informed about emerging threats and vulnerabilities that could affect the organization.

Detecting and responding to security breaches is a critical capability for software teams in today's cybersecurity landscape. By implementing effective detection strategies, establishing a structured response plan, and leveraging the right tools and resources, organizations can minimize the impact of security incidents and enhance their overall security posture. Continuous training, regular testing, and iterative improvements to incident response practices are essential for adapting to the evolving threat landscape. By fostering a culture of security awareness and preparedness, software teams can ensure that they are equipped to handle breaches swiftly and effectively, ultimately protecting their systems, data, and reputation.

11.3 Patch Management and Applying Security Updates

In the realm of software development and IT security, patch management and timely application of security updates are critical components of maintaining a secure environment. Vulnerabilities in software can lead to unauthorized access, data breaches, and other security incidents if not properly addressed. This section delves into the significance of patch management, best practices for implementing security updates, and strategies to ensure that systems remain secure and resilient against emerging threats.

1. Understanding Patch Management

Definition:

Patch management refers to the process of identifying, acquiring, testing, and installing patches (or updates) for software applications and systems to fix vulnerabilities, enhance functionality, or improve performance. This is crucial for both operating systems and applications, as unpatched software can serve as an entry point for attackers.

Importance of Patch Management:

- **Mitigating Security Risks**: Regularly applying patches can significantly reduce the risk of exploitation by addressing known vulnerabilities before they can be targeted.
- **Compliance Requirements**: Many regulatory standards and industry frameworks require organizations to maintain up-to-date systems as part of their compliance efforts.
- **Improving System Stability**: Beyond security, patches often include bug fixes and performance improvements that enhance the overall stability and usability of software.
- **Protecting Reputation**: A proactive approach to patch management helps organizations maintain customer trust by demonstrating a commitment to security.

2. The Patch Management Process

An effective patch management process involves several key steps to ensure that patches are applied systematically and securely:

Inventory Management:

- **Asset Identification**: Maintain an inventory of all hardware and software assets within the organization. This includes operating systems, applications, network devices, and third-party software.
- **Vulnerability Assessment**: Regularly conduct vulnerability assessments to identify systems that are missing critical updates or are known to be susceptible to exploits.

Patch Identification:

- **Source Updates**: Monitor vendors and software providers for announcements regarding new patches and updates. Utilize official channels, such as security bulletins, mailing lists, or vendor websites.
- **Prioritize Patches**: Evaluate patches based on severity and criticality. Focus on those that address high-risk vulnerabilities that could lead to severe consequences if exploited.

Testing Patches:

- **Establish a Testing Environment**: Create a controlled testing environment that mirrors the production environment to evaluate patches before deployment. This helps identify potential conflicts and issues.
- **Conduct Testing**: Test patches for functionality, compatibility, and performance. This step helps ensure that the application or system will remain stable after the patch is applied.

Deployment of Patches:

- **Scheduling Updates**: Develop a schedule for deploying patches to minimize disruption to operations. This may involve routine maintenance windows or rolling updates for critical systems.
- **Automated Patch Management Tools**: Consider using automated patch management solutions that can streamline the deployment process and reduce manual efforts.

Verification and Monitoring:

- **Confirm Patch Installation**: After deployment, verify that patches have been successfully installed and are functioning as expected. This may involve running scripts or checks to ensure compliance.
- **Ongoing Monitoring**: Continuously monitor systems for signs of vulnerabilities or anomalies post-patch. Regularly review logs and conduct scans to detect potential issues.

Documentation and Reporting:

- **Maintain Records**: Document all patch management activities, including patch identification, testing, deployment, and verification. This provides a historical record for compliance and auditing purposes.
- **Reporting to Stakeholders**: Communicate patch status and security updates to relevant stakeholders, ensuring that management and IT teams are informed of potential risks and mitigation efforts.

3. Best Practices for Patch Management

Establish a Patch Management Policy:

Develop a comprehensive patch management policy that outlines procedures, responsibilities, and timelines for patching. Ensure that all team members understand their roles in the process.

Prioritize Critical Systems:

Identify and prioritize critical systems and applications that require immediate attention when vulnerabilities are discovered. This ensures that the most significant risks are addressed promptly.

Automate Where Possible:

Leverage automation tools to streamline the patch management process. Automated patch management solutions can significantly reduce manual efforts and minimize the risk of human error.

Regularly Review and Update Policies:

Periodically review and update the patch management policy to reflect changes in the technology landscape, new threats, and organizational needs. This ensures that the process remains effective and relevant.

Train Employees:

Provide ongoing training for IT staff and relevant personnel on the importance of patch management and secure coding practices. This fosters a culture of security awareness within the organization.

Create a Rollback Plan:

Develop a rollback plan in case a patch causes unforeseen issues or conflicts. This allows for quick recovery and minimizes downtime in the event of problems.

4. Tools for Effective Patch Management

Patch Management Software:

Utilize specialized software to streamline the patch management process. Popular options include:

- **Microsoft System Center Configuration Manager (SCCM):** This tool helps automate the deployment of patches across Windows environments.
- **ManageEngine Patch Manager Plus**: This software provides automated patch management for various operating systems and applications.

Vulnerability Scanning Tools:

Implement vulnerability scanning solutions to identify systems that require patches. Common tools include:

- **Qualys Vulnerability Management**: A cloud-based service that provides continuous vulnerability scanning and assessment.
- **Nessus**: A widely used vulnerability scanner that helps identify vulnerabilities across various systems.

Asset Management Solutions:

Maintain an accurate inventory of software and hardware assets using asset management tools, such as:

- **ServiceNow**: Provides a comprehensive asset management solution integrated with incident and change management.
- **Lansweeper**: Offers network inventory management capabilities to identify all devices on the network.

Effective patch management and timely application of security updates are essential practices for maintaining a secure software environment. By establishing a systematic patch management process, organizations can mitigate risks associated with unpatched vulnerabilities and enhance their overall security posture. Regular assessments, automated tools, and well-defined policies are critical components of a successful patch management strategy. As cyber threats continue to evolve, organizations must remain vigilant and proactive in their approach to patch management, ensuring that they protect their systems and sensitive data from potential exploitation. By fostering a culture of security awareness and continuous improvement, software teams can significantly reduce their exposure to risks and respond effectively to emerging threats.

12. Security Challenges and Emerging Threats

In Security Challenges and Emerging Threats, we examine the ever-evolving landscape of cybersecurity, highlighting the latest challenges that developers and organizations face in securing their software. This chapter discusses various emerging threats, such as supply chain attacks, ransomware, and the implications of artificial intelligence on security, exploring how these risks can exploit vulnerabilities in software systems. We also emphasize the importance of staying informed about current trends and threat intelligence to proactively defend against potential attacks. Additionally, we discuss strategies for fostering a culture of security awareness within development teams, encouraging continuous education and training to adapt to new threats. By understanding and addressing these security challenges, developers can build more resilient applications that are better equipped to withstand the complexities of the modern threat landscape.

12.1 Addressing Supply Chain Attacks and Dependency Security

In the modern software development landscape, supply chain attacks have become a significant concern for organizations worldwide. As software systems increasingly rely on third-party components, libraries, and services, vulnerabilities within these dependencies can lead to catastrophic security breaches. This section explores the nature of supply chain attacks, the challenges they pose, and best practices for securing dependencies to protect software applications and systems from exploitation.

1. Understanding Supply Chain Attacks

Definition:

A supply chain attack occurs when an adversary targets a less secure element in a software supply chain to compromise a system. This could involve exploiting vulnerabilities in third-party libraries, injecting malicious code into software updates, or breaching vendors that provide essential components.

Types of Supply Chain Attacks:

- **Code Injection**: Attackers may inject malicious code into open-source libraries or software updates, which, when integrated into applications, compromise the overall system.
- **Trojanized Software**: Legitimate software may be altered by attackers before it reaches the end user, embedding vulnerabilities or backdoors that can be exploited later.
- **Dependency Confusion**: This occurs when an attacker uploads a malicious package to a public repository that has the same name as a legitimate private package, tricking the package manager into downloading the malicious version.

2. The Rise of Supply Chain Attacks

Recent high-profile incidents, such as the SolarWinds attack and the Codecov breach, have highlighted the vulnerability of software supply chains. These events demonstrated how attackers could exploit trusted relationships within the supply chain to gain unauthorized access to sensitive information or systems. The increased reliance on third-party components, especially open-source libraries, makes software supply chains an attractive target for cybercriminals.

3. Challenges in Dependency Security

Organizations face several challenges when it comes to securing software dependencies:

Complexity of Dependencies: Modern applications often depend on a vast array of libraries and components, making it difficult to track and manage all dependencies effectively. Each dependency can introduce vulnerabilities.

Rapid Software Development: The pace of software development often prioritizes speed over security. Developers may integrate third-party libraries without fully vetting their security practices or history.

Limited Visibility: Organizations often lack visibility into their software supply chains. It can be challenging to know where components originate, how they are maintained, and whether they have known vulnerabilities.

Open Source Risks: Open-source libraries, while offering many benefits, can also pose risks if they are not adequately maintained or if their maintainers do not follow secure coding practices.

4. Best Practices for Securing Dependencies

To mitigate the risks associated with supply chain attacks, organizations should implement the following best practices for dependency security:

Conduct Dependency Inventory and Risk Assessment:

- **Maintain an Inventory**: Keep a detailed inventory of all third-party libraries and dependencies used within applications. This includes tracking versions and licenses.
- **Perform Risk Assessments**: Evaluate the security posture of dependencies by considering factors such as the library's popularity, frequency of updates, known vulnerabilities, and the reputation of its maintainers.

Implement a Software Bill of Materials (SBOM):

- **What is SBOM?:** An SBOM is a comprehensive inventory of all components, libraries, and dependencies included in a software product. It provides transparency regarding the origins and versions of all components.
- **Benefits**: SBOMs enhance visibility into software supply chains and enable organizations to respond more effectively to vulnerabilities. They help track which components need updating and facilitate compliance with regulatory requirements.

Use Trusted Sources and Repositories:

- **Verify Sources**: Only download and integrate libraries from reputable sources and official repositories. Verify the authenticity of packages and maintainers to reduce the risk of dependency confusion and code injection attacks.
- **Use Package Management Best Practices**: Employ package management tools that verify checksums or signatures to ensure the integrity of downloaded components.

Automate Dependency Management:

- **Dependency Scanning Tools**: Use tools like OWASP Dependency-Check, Snyk, or Black Duck to automate the scanning of dependencies for known vulnerabilities. These tools help identify outdated or vulnerable components in real time.
- **Continuous Monitoring**: Implement continuous monitoring to track dependencies for new vulnerabilities and ensure timely updates.

Adopt a Secure Development Lifecycle (SDLC):

- **Integrate Security Early**: Embed security practices within the development process. This includes conducting threat modeling and risk assessments during the design phase and regularly testing dependencies throughout the development lifecycle.
- **Code Reviews and Static Analysis**: Implement code reviews and static analysis to detect potential security issues in dependencies, particularly when integrating new libraries.

Establish Incident Response Procedures:

- **Response Plan**: Develop a clear incident response plan for handling supply chain attacks and vulnerabilities in dependencies. This should include procedures for identifying, assessing, and mitigating the impact of a breach.
- **Communication Protocols**: Establish communication protocols for informing relevant stakeholders, including developers, management, and customers, in the event of a security incident.

5. Tools and Resources for Dependency Security

Dependency Management Tools:

- **Maven, Gradle, npm**: Utilize modern package managers that offer features for managing dependencies and ensuring their integrity.
- **Artifactory, Nexus**: Use repository managers to control and secure access to dependencies, preventing unauthorized packages from being included in builds.

Vulnerability Scanning Solutions:

- **Snyk**: A popular tool for identifying and fixing vulnerabilities in open-source libraries and dependencies.
- **WhiteSource**: Provides real-time security alerts for open-source vulnerabilities and helps automate patching processes.

SBOM Generation Tools:

- **CycloneDX**: A lightweight SBOM standard that helps organizations create and share component inventories.
- **SPDX**: The Software Package Data Exchange (SPDX) provides a standard format for sharing information about software components and their licenses.

As supply chain attacks continue to pose significant threats to software security, organizations must prioritize dependency security as part of their overall security strategy. By implementing best practices such as maintaining an inventory of dependencies, using trusted sources, automating vulnerability scanning, and establishing incident response procedures, organizations can significantly reduce the risk of compromise. The proactive management of software supply chains is essential for ensuring the integrity and security of applications in an increasingly interconnected digital landscape. As threats evolve, ongoing vigilance and a commitment to secure coding practices will be key to safeguarding systems and data from exploitation.

12.2 Emerging Threats: AI and Machine Learning Security Risks

Artificial Intelligence (AI) and Machine Learning (ML) have become integral to modern software applications, enabling enhanced automation, improved decision-making, and personalized experiences. However, as organizations increasingly adopt these technologies, they also face a new set of security risks and challenges. This section explores the emerging threats associated with AI and ML, examining how they can be exploited and what measures can be taken to mitigate these risks.

1. Understanding AI and ML Security Risks

AI and ML Overview:

AI encompasses a range of technologies that simulate human intelligence, while ML specifically focuses on algorithms that enable systems to learn from data and improve over time. These technologies are used in various applications, including fraud detection, autonomous systems, natural language processing, and more.

Security Risks:

While AI and ML can enhance security efforts, they also introduce new vulnerabilities that can be exploited by attackers. Some of the primary security risks include:

Adversarial Attacks:

Adversarial attacks involve manipulating input data to deceive AI and ML models into making incorrect predictions or classifications. For example, an attacker might alter an image in such a way that a facial recognition system misidentifies the subject.

- **Techniques**: Common techniques include adding noise, changing pixel values, or creating misleading data samples that exploit weaknesses in the model.
- **Impact**: Successful adversarial attacks can undermine the reliability of AI systems, leading to incorrect decisions or actions that can have serious consequences.

Data Poisoning:

In data poisoning attacks, an adversary injects malicious or misleading data into the training set of a machine learning model. This can result in the model learning incorrect patterns, making it less effective or even harmful.

- **Examples**: For instance, in a fraud detection system, attackers could submit fraudulent transactions that are designed to appear legitimate, thus skewing the model's learning process.
- **Consequences**: Data poisoning can degrade the accuracy of AI models, leading to poor decision-making and increased vulnerabilities in systems reliant on those models.

Model Inversion:

Model inversion attacks enable attackers to infer sensitive information about the training data by exploiting the outputs of a machine learning model. This is particularly concerning in scenarios where AI models are trained on sensitive personal data.

- **How It Works**: By observing the model's predictions, attackers can reconstruct input data, potentially revealing confidential information.
- **Risks**: Model inversion can lead to data breaches and privacy violations, making it essential to safeguard sensitive information used in training.

Unauthorized Model Access:

The accessibility of machine learning models raises concerns about unauthorized use or theft. Attackers may attempt to reverse-engineer proprietary models to replicate or manipulate their functionality for malicious purposes.

Implications: Theft of AI models can lead to intellectual property theft, loss of competitive advantage, and unauthorized access to sensitive systems.

Overfitting and Model Robustness:

If a machine learning model is overfitted to the training data, it may perform poorly when encountering new, unseen data. Attackers can exploit this lack of robustness to manipulate inputs and cause the model to fail.

Impact: An overfitted model is less adaptable and can be more easily tricked by adversaries, leading to security vulnerabilities.

2. The Implications of AI and ML Security Risks

The security risks associated with AI and ML can have far-reaching consequences for organizations, including:

Financial Loss:

Breaches resulting from exploited AI vulnerabilities can lead to significant financial losses, whether from direct theft, regulatory fines, or reputational damage.

Loss of Trust:

Users and customers may lose trust in AI-driven systems if they perceive them as insecure or prone to manipulation. This can damage an organization's reputation and lead to decreased user adoption.

Regulatory Compliance Issues:

Organizations using AI and ML technologies must comply with data protection regulations (e.g., GDPR, CCPA). Failures resulting from AI security vulnerabilities can lead to compliance violations and associated penalties.

Operational Disruption:

Exploiting AI vulnerabilities can lead to operational disruptions, particularly in critical systems that rely on AI for decision-making. This can impact service availability and organizational efficiency.

3. Best Practices for Securing AI and ML Systems

To address the security risks associated with AI and ML, organizations should implement several best practices:

Robust Model Training:

- **Diverse Data Sets**: Use diverse and representative training data to improve model resilience. This helps prevent overfitting and reduces the model's susceptibility to adversarial attacks.
- **Regular Model Updates**: Continuously update models with new data to ensure they adapt to evolving patterns and threats.

Implementing Adversarial Training:

- **Adversarial Examples**: Incorporate adversarial examples into the training process. This helps models learn to recognize and mitigate potential adversarial inputs.
- **Testing for Vulnerabilities**: Regularly test models against known adversarial techniques to assess their robustness and identify weaknesses.

Data Integrity Measures:

- **Data Validation**: Implement data validation and sanitization processes to prevent data poisoning. Ensure that input data is clean and verified before being used in training or inference.
- **Access Controls**: Establish strict access controls to limit who can modify training data and models, reducing the risk of unauthorized data manipulation.

Privacy-Preserving Techniques:

- **Differential Privacy**: Employ differential privacy techniques to protect sensitive data used in training. This allows models to learn from data without exposing individual data points.
- **Federated Learning**: Use federated learning to train models across decentralized devices without sharing sensitive data, enhancing privacy and security.

Regular Audits and Monitoring:

- **Security Audits**: Conduct regular security audits of AI and ML systems to identify vulnerabilities and ensure compliance with security policies.
- **Anomaly Detection**: Implement monitoring tools that can detect unusual patterns or behavior in AI models, allowing for timely intervention in the event of a potential attack.

Establish an Incident Response Plan:

- **Preparedness**: Develop an incident response plan specific to AI and ML security incidents. This plan should outline procedures for identifying, assessing, and responding to AI-related threats.
- **Training and Awareness**: Train personnel on recognizing AI-related security risks and responding effectively to incidents.

As organizations increasingly rely on AI and machine learning technologies, the security risks associated with these systems cannot be overlooked. Adversarial attacks, data poisoning, and model inversion represent just a few of the threats that can exploit the unique vulnerabilities of AI. By adopting best practices, including robust model training, data integrity measures, and incident response planning, organizations can mitigate these risks and enhance the security of their AI and ML applications. Continuous vigilance, monitoring, and adaptation to the evolving threat landscape are essential for safeguarding against emerging threats in the rapidly changing world of AI and machine learning. By addressing these challenges proactively, organizations can harness the power of AI while ensuring the security and integrity of their systems and data.

12.3 Building a Culture of Security Awareness in Development Teams

In today's fast-paced software development environment, cultivating a culture of security awareness within development teams is paramount. As cyber threats become increasingly sophisticated and prevalent, ensuring that every member of the team understands security principles, practices, and responsibilities can significantly reduce vulnerabilities in software applications. This section outlines the importance of security awareness, the components of an effective security culture, and practical strategies for embedding security consciousness in development teams.

1. The Importance of Security Awareness

Understanding the Landscape:

Cybersecurity incidents can have severe repercussions for organizations, including financial losses, reputational damage, and legal implications. With the rapid evolution of threats, security cannot be the sole responsibility of a designated team; it must be ingrained in every aspect of the development process.

Empowering Team Members:

When developers and other stakeholders understand security principles, they can proactively identify and address potential vulnerabilities during the design and development phases. This empowerment reduces the risk of security flaws and enhances overall software quality.

2. Components of a Security Culture

Shared Responsibility:

Security should be viewed as a collective responsibility rather than the duty of a specific role or team. Every member of the development team, from developers to project managers, should recognize their role in maintaining security.

Continuous Learning:

A culture of security awareness thrives on continuous education and training. Teams should regularly update their knowledge about emerging threats, best practices, and tools for secure development.

Open Communication:

Fostering an environment where team members feel comfortable discussing security concerns, reporting vulnerabilities, and sharing knowledge is crucial. Open communication encourages collaboration and ensures that security is a priority.

Recognition and Rewards:

Recognizing and rewarding team members who actively contribute to security efforts can motivate others to adopt secure practices. Celebrating successes reinforces the importance of security awareness.

Integration with Development Practices:

Security should be integrated into the software development lifecycle (SDLC) rather than treated as an afterthought. By embedding security practices into daily workflows, teams can cultivate a security-focused mindset.

3. Strategies for Building Security Awareness

Regular Training and Workshops:

- **Security Training Sessions**: Conduct regular training sessions to educate team members about secure coding practices, threat modeling, and risk assessment. Tailor training to specific roles within the development team, ensuring relevance and effectiveness.
- **Hands-On Workshops**: Organize hands-on workshops where developers can practice secure coding techniques and learn about common vulnerabilities (e.g., SQL injection, cross-site scripting). Real-world scenarios help reinforce theoretical knowledge.

Implement Security Champions:

- **Designating Security Champions**: Identify and appoint security champions within development teams. These individuals serve as advocates for security, helping to disseminate knowledge, provide guidance, and encourage secure practices among their peers.
- **Peer Learning**: Security champions can facilitate peer learning sessions, where team members can share experiences, challenges, and solutions related to security.

Create Clear Documentation and Resources:

- **Security Guidelines**: Develop clear, accessible security guidelines and best practices for developers. This documentation should cover secure coding standards, common vulnerabilities, and procedures for reporting security issues.
- **Knowledge Base**: Create a centralized knowledge base that team members can refer to for security-related questions and resources. This can include links to relevant articles, tools, and training materials.

Incorporate Security in Agile Practices:

- **Security User Stories**: In Agile development environments, incorporate security-related user stories into sprints. This ensures that security considerations are addressed during planning and development.
- **Regular Reviews and Retrospectives**: Include security reviews in sprint retrospectives to evaluate the team's performance in terms of security practices and identify areas for improvement.

Conduct Security Assessments and Simulations:

- **Penetration Testing**: Regularly conduct penetration tests and security assessments to evaluate the security posture of applications. Involve development teams in the process to help them understand vulnerabilities and remediation techniques.
- **Red Team Exercises**: Simulate real-world attacks through red team exercises to help teams experience firsthand the tactics and techniques employed by adversaries. This can enhance their understanding of potential threats and reinforce the importance of security.

Establish Metrics and Feedback Loops:

- **Security Metrics**: Track and analyze security metrics, such as the number of vulnerabilities identified and resolved, to assess the effectiveness of security initiatives. Share these metrics with the team to create awareness and drive improvement.
- **Feedback Mechanisms**: Implement feedback mechanisms, such as surveys or one-on-one discussions, to gather insights from team members about security practices, training effectiveness, and areas for improvement.

Building a culture of security awareness in development teams is not a one-time effort but an ongoing commitment that requires active participation from all team members. By fostering a shared sense of responsibility, providing continuous training, and integrating security into development practices, organizations can significantly reduce the risk of vulnerabilities in their software applications. A security-aware culture not only enhances the overall quality of software but also empowers teams to respond effectively to emerging threats in a rapidly changing cybersecurity landscape. In the end, a strong security culture is a cornerstone of resilient software development and an essential component of any organization's cybersecurity strategy.

In **Building Secure Software: A Hands-On Guide for Developers**, security expert *Nikolai Lebedev* delivers a comprehensive, practical approach to embedding security at every stage of software development. As digital threats grow in sophistication and frequency, secure software development has become essential. This guide equips developers with the principles, techniques, and real-world tools needed to protect their applications from vulnerabilities and build resilient, trustworthy systems.

Through twelve carefully crafted chapters, readers will learn how to incorporate secure coding standards, perform effective threat modeling, and implement robust encryption practices. From securing APIs and web applications to mastering DevSecOps and proactive incident response, each chapter provides hands-on advice, actionable techniques, and insights drawn from industry best practices. With a focus on practical application, this book transforms complex security concepts into accessible steps that developers can integrate into their daily workflows.

Whether you're a beginner in secure software practices or a seasoned developer looking to enhance your security skills, Building Secure Software is an essential resource. This book is your step-by-step guide to building software that stands strong against evolving threats—offering a foundation for security and confidence in every line of code you write.

www.ingramcontent.com/pod-product-compliance
Lightning Source LLC
Chambersburg PA
CBHW062106220526
45471CB00010B/3614